THE ART OF GOLF

THE ART OF GOLF
A Year With Saul

R.A YEAGER

Published in the United States of America

ISBN 978-1-953904-10-2 (SC)

R.A. Yeager Publishing
222 West 6th Street
Suite 400, San Pedro, CA, 90731
www.stellarliterary.com

Ordering Information and Rights Permission:
Quantity sales. Special discounts might be available on
quantity purchases by corporations, associations, and others.
For details, contact the publisher at the address above.

For Book Rights Adaptation and other Rights Permission. Call us at
toll free 1-888-945-8513 or send us email at admin@stellarliteray.com.

CONTENTS

PREFACE

I started writing what is enclosed in these pages as an instructional piece on golf from my years as a caddie, assistant, and close friend of Solomon Good. Well into my writing, I realized that the theory of golf, what Saul conveyed to me, was only part who he was. Knowing him as a person, outside of teaching and competition, is critical to understanding his entire philosophy on the Art of Golf.

As you read this story, there will be parts that are excerpts from my instructional book. If you're interested in evolving your own theory of golf, I'll be glad to provide the instructional lesson plan that Saul gave to Dom.

I hope you enjoy reading this story as much I did living it.

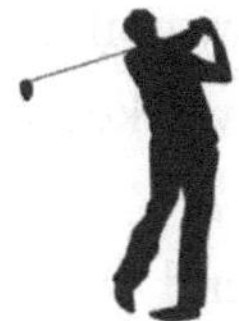

CHAPTER 1

Dominic Ciacchini, Dom to his friends, sat in the men's grill at his club, drinking with friends. The place was old money which, in those parts, meant a lot of exposed oak and cherry wood in an English Tudor clubhouse. As I said, Dom was talking with his friends. What all of them had in common was that they were all seriously rich. When I say rich, I mean the kind that pay in taxes what some millionaires make a year. Dom was a well-built, good-looking man with a funny outlook on life, except when he was drinking with his buds. That was one thing about Dom: if he got loaded, he would never back down from a bet.

This golf club was one with few strictly social

members and Dom was one of them. He didn't play golf, even though all of his friends did. He would be there, ready to shoot the shit with them after their rounds. On this particular night, he got to shooting off his mouth about how golf *isn't that hard*. He claims that in one year, if he worked on the game, he would beat anyone there.

Woody is an ex-friend who carries a four handicap and would be better if he wasn't so clueless about how to play a course. Well, he ended up saying the one word that set everything in motion: "bullshit." At the end of the day, they ended up betting huge dollars on who was right, rules were set up, and the bet began.

Dom goes to his office the next morning, tells his next-in-command that he's in charge for the next year and takes the year off. The bet is worth much less than what either of them makes a year. Dom and Woody had a history, though, and neither one of them were about to back off from an opportunity to best the other.

Not many knew what the history between them consisted of. The ones who thought they did, never spoke of it. They were probably all scared of Dom, whether they would admit it or not. It was obvious there was something pretty big because the hatred ran deep. There was also a huge gash on the right side of Dom's face, covered by his beard. No one knew how he got it, but it definitely had something to do with the thing between him and Woody.

The next day, Dom was on a flight to Pinehurst.

He went there to find a golf instructor name Solomon Good. Everyone thought that was his nom de plume, but no one knew for sure. What they did know is that *if* you can get him to teach you, you must do whatever is necessary to get on his calendar.

He did not teach many people. Money alone did not guarantee you any of his time. If you were serious about the game, though, and could convince him that you would do whatever it takes to be really good, he may take you on.

Now, that didn't mean he could be had for a good story. He charged those who had money a lot. How much, I can't say. That was his number one rule, and everyone knew it: Never talk to anyone about him or about the time you spent with him. That includes the price you paid to be a student of his. Break this rule and you're not his student anymore.

If you didn't have money, he would take you on for nothing but the desire to be great, and you would do whatever in return for his help. This applied especially to children. God, did he love kids that loved golf.

If you were able to get in with him, all it took was one strike and you're out. If you were lazy and didn't work hard on what he told you to do, and he would know at the next lesson how hard you'd worked, he'd just walk. I have seen him do it before and, man, is it something.

One day, he was on the tee with this big guy: WWE wrestler kind of big. The guy made a comment about not having time to work on something as Saul had instructed. Saul just nodded his head, turned, and walked away. Thirty minutes later, Saul's with a 13-year-old kid that can seriously play, not fifty yards away from where he left this guy, dumfounded.

Big guy obviously didn't like what was going on and that's where it got weird. He walked up to Saul and started speaking loudly. He was not happy. It went on for about a minute then Saul looked that guy right in the eye. I'm thinking: some shit's going to go down. I got up and started towards them and was about five yards away when I saw it. The look Saul gave this guy scared me half to death and it wasn't even for me. Big man's about ready to shit himself. All from a stare; just one fucking look! Can you believe that? Well now that I saw it, I do. The guy couldn't walk away fast enough, apologizing the whole way, even when no one could hear him.

I busted out laughing. I couldn't stop myself. I looked at Saul and he shot me a quick smile then went back to teaching the kid. Saul never laughed when he was teaching. He would talk to himself all day under his breath, but when he was teaching, he selected his words carefully. It was business and the course was his office. He was really a funny guy and could get me laughing all night long, but no one knew him like that, except me.

You can call me Blu.

Blaise Tyre Jones is my given name. Blaise was from my mom. She said her and my dad fell in love, got married, and then pregnant so fast it was like a blazing wildfire. My dad loved golf and Bobby Jones so that's how I got the rest of my name. Part of my dad's love for Jones, I thought, had to do with the fact that we shared his last name. I later realized it was because of who Bobby Jones was and the respect he showed everyone. He was like Arnie, before Arnie.

The name Blu came from Saul. I wasn't sure why he called me that at first, but I liked it. Pretty soon, everyone called me that.

I grew up in the sand hills of North Carolina, not far from Pinehurst. My parents were my best friends. My dad was ex-army and taught me patience, perseverance, and hard work. My mother taught me lots of things that a lot of people considered women's work. She taught me to cook, to sew and to keep my room clean. I loved spending time with both of them, so it was easy to learn whatever they wanted to teach me.

Respect was everything to my dad. Respect for others, respect for the game, and always respect for your family. It was a trait I picked up early on. He told me that, if there is something or someone I didn't respect, I was to leave it be, walk away, and never say anything about it. "If you don't like them, then you aint gonna change them," he'd say. "Let 'em be."

When I was growing up, I thought my life was perfect. I had two friends in high school that I'd hung with since ninth grade. Doug was an outgoing guy, kind of a player. Clay was my other friend. We called him Race because his last name was Bannon. He only hung out with us.

Clay was an orphan and stayed with a foster family pretty close to my house. We played basketball together in high school and golf in the fall while Doug played football. The strange thing about Clay was that he looked a lot like me. Classmates called us "The Twins." I didn't really pay much attention to it. We were best friends and neither of us had any others. It's not like we were picked on or anything; we just kept to ourselves.

So, as I said, I thought my life was relatively perfect. That was, until Spring of my senior year; March 28th of 1998, to be exact. My parents went out to the store and, on the way home, got sideswiped by another car. The collision sent them barreling straight into a tree, head on. They both died at the scene. I was told about the accident by a local deputy whom I had known for years. He drove me to the morgue to see them and brought me home after. I was dizzy, like in a dream. I functioned throughout my day, but mindlessly, like a zombie.

Al, my godfather, was waiting at the house when I got home. He talked with me that night and stayed with me for the next week. I was so lost, and he could see it. I went back to school to finish out my last semester and got my diploma.

A week after graduation, I was out partying with Clay and Doug and we were all a little drunk. Doug had driven. He usually drove because my truck was full of tools from some light construction jobs I did on the side. It was work I used to do with my dad.

Doug had dropped me off at home and about 20 minutes later, I got a call from him. He told me to come down the street to Clay's house; that he needed help.

He sounded so scared. I went to my pick up and drove as fast as I could. I saw his Doug's truck on the side of the road with the lights still on. Clay lived down a long dirt road in the country with no houses on it, but his. I pulled off the road and walked up to Doug who was staring at the side of the road. When I got up next to him, I saw Clay. He was lying in the ditch, covered in blood. He wasn't moving.

I looked at Doug, who was still staring down at the ditch.

"What happened, Doug?" I asked.

"He just was there," he said softly. "I didn't even see him. I dropped him off, back there, about 40 yards or so." He was pointing down towards Clay's house, but his eyes still hadn't left the ditch. Doug explained, "He said he wanted to finish his beer before going to his house, so I drove to the end of the street to turn around. On the way back, I didn't see him. I just I didn't see him." Doug was crying now.

I looked at Clay. "Get it together," I said. "We can cry together, later. Right now, we gotta decide. Call the cops or handle all this right now."

I looked back at him, but he didn't say anything.

"Look, you broke up with the chief's daughter a

week before prom and that was less than a month ago. If you ask me, I say we take care of this right now."

Doug nodded and mumbled, "Okay."

I went to my truck, pulled out a bunch of tools and grabbed the tarp that was under them. I walked past Doug and down to where Clay's body was, laying the tarp out next to him. Doug was still in shock, just standing there staring at our friend's body. I shook him out of it by yelling, "Doug!" Then, a bit quieter, "Get your ass down here." We rolled up Clay's body in the tarp and carried him to the back of Doug's truck. I told him to follow me and started driving down route 211 West to my godfather's farm. Al owned about a thousand acres in total. We pulled off 211 and drove about a mile down the road onto his driveway. I drove past the house and the barn, down a long dirt road and into to a small back section of field.

It was about two acres and not attached to any of the other fields. Al had sharecroppers farm the land, but he kept this section to farm himself when he wanted to. We drove to the back, near a grove of magnolia trees and turned my truck towards the field. I grabbed a shovel out of the bed and found a place to start digging. I scooped a few heaps of dirt out of the ground and then handed the shovel to Doug.

He started going at it, fast and hard, then stopped to catch his breath. He looked at me, resting his arm on the handle.

"Why are you doing this?" he asked.

"Man, two months ago, I had five people in my life that I consider family. Right now, you and my godfather are all that's left, and Mr. Williams won't be around forever. You take this to the police and the they will bury you, himself. Then, when Al dies, I'll be completely alone. I won't have nobody."

Then, I heard a snap of a twig behind me. A flashlight hit us both in the eyes, blinding us. The light lowered a bit and I shielded my eyes with my hand. I saw it was my godfather, Mr. Williams.

"Hi boys." He focused the light on where we were digging. "Do I want to know?"

I stood up. "Sir, I don't believe you do."

"Okay, then tell me. Was it an accident?"

Doug spoke right up, "Yes! Sir, it was my fault, but it was an accident. I didn't…"

"Okay, then," Al cut him off, "I'll get another shovel from the barn. You make damn sure you dig it deep. Don't want no animals getting curious some night." He turned to walk to the barn, then stopped. "Boys, one more thing. This is your two acres to farm, now. I expect you to do it right, from planting to harvest and everything in between. You see, some of the others might try to grab it for themselves if it goes unattended for too long. We wouldn't want that, would we?"

"No sir," we spoke in unison.

About two months after that night, I got a call from Mrs. Rayburn. She was Clay's foster mom and a real sweet lady. She asked me to come over whenever I was free. I told her I would be right over.

I drove to Ms. Rayburn's house and I passed the place on the road where Clay died. By the time I had put my truck in park at the Rayburns, I was openly crying. I must have been sitting there for a bit because the truck door opened all of a sudden and Ms. Rayburn leaned in and held me. I quickly got myself together from the shock, as well as the shame. As a man, I shouldn't be seen crying. It seemed wrong. She was whispering in my ear like Mom used to, "It's okay son, let it out. We miss him, too."

For a second, I had forgotten that they still thought Clay ran away, not that he was dead. I got out of the truck and walked with her towards the house. She offered me some lemonade from a pitcher she had sitting on the table between two porch chairs.

We sat down and made small talk for minute before she changed the subject by asking, "Did you know Clay was unhappy here? Did he ever say anything to you about running away?"

"No ma'am, as matter of fact, I thought we were close, like family. I – I don't know."

With that she reached over and held my hand in hers. "We did too, sugar." A moment later she reached down, beside her chair, and with both hands, grabbed a two large envelopes. She handed it to me. As I moved to open it, she stopped me, saying, "Blaise, you can look at it later. It's all of Clay's papers: his birth certificate, social security card, and all the likes. I thought, maybe, if he ever came through here again, he would probably look you up, first. He could probably get duplicates, but if you ever see him, well, you know."

I shook my head and agreed, "I will, if I ever do." As I was walking back to my truck, she yelled out, "Blaise, if you ever want to stop over for dinner, we would like that a lot. Mr. Rayburn loved talking sports with you boys."

"Ma'am, I will soon," I said. "I'm still just trying to get my balance since, well, you know."

I got back to my house and started going through the contents of the envelope. Like she said, there was his birth certificate, his driver's license, and a social security card. Then, I came across some papers about his foster care. He had lived in six different places since he was five years old. There were some newspaper clippings about his parents. It said they were murdered, along with his sister, in a home invasion. The article went on to talk about how Clayton had seen the whole thing while hiding in a closet. Clay had never told us, and we never asked. I started to cry again.

I looked at his old license, again. I held mine up next to it and finally saw what everyone was saying about us being twins. We did look a whole lot alike. I gathered up all the stuff that I had taken from the envelope and put it all back. I then put the envelope in a desk drawer and made a mental note to take care of it later. That was twenty years ago.

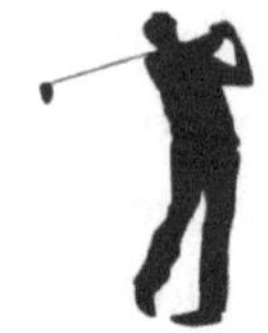

CHAPTER 2

Anyway, like I said, no one got close to Saul, but me. I was his friend, maybe his only friend. I'm the only one who knew exactly how funny this guy was. He wasn't like that with anyone else. He had a sharp, quick wit and a mind that saw everything differently than others. It got to the point where something would happen and he would just look at me, and I'd smile because I knew what he was thinking.

I am not sure why he picked me, but I'm glad he did. I had heard of him before I ever met him. Everything I'd heard was obscure; a third or fourth-hand story about him at this course or that tournament. It was strange because it seemed like either no one had a firsthand account of what he was really like, or they were all too scared to repeat it.

One day I was caddying at Pinehurst #2 and he walks up to the caddie master, asks him where he could find me. How he even knew my name was just the beginning of things that I didn't understand. I'm just a caddie, making a good living, that's never looped regularly for a tour player, or a great golfer, for that matter. I carried in a couple of tour events, but for no one that's anybody you've heard of.

So, I'm on the practice tee with my players for the day and he walks up and says, "You Jones?" I told him I was. I shook his hand and said, "Blaise Jones, sir." Holding on to my hand, he looked me in eye and said, "Okay, I need ya' at Mid Pines, tomorrow at 9 a.m. on the putting green. You good with that?" I told him I was. He turned and said, "I'll see you then, Blu."

I stood there trying to figure out what had just happened. First off, who the hell is *Blu*? Then I realized, he never actually told me who he was. I knew, but it was still weird. It wasn't like he was so into himself that he'd assumed I'd know who he was. It was more like he didn't care, and he'd see me tomorrow. Like I said, it was just plain weird. But that kind of goes along with what I'd heard about him.

I parked in the back of the lot when I arrived at Mid Pines. Today was the Hickory Tournament meaning everyone played with clubs and balls from the hickory shafted club era, pre 1910. I walked into the pro shop and saw Jack, one of the assistant pros at the club who I knew. I asked him if he'd seen Mr. Good.

"Oh, yeah, he's out there, standing at the putting green, watching." Jack pointed out onto the course and said, "He's been in that spot for the last half-hour." I asked when we were on the tee and he told me 11:50 on number 10. I looked at him, confused. "Yeah, I know," he said, shaking his head.

I walked out from the shop towards the green. Saul was three hours early. Nobody shows up that long before a tee time in a tournament. I knew right then that this was no ordinary loop.

I saw him standing there and just watched him. He was dressed in plus fours, knickers with long socks, a dress shirt, and a tie, covered by a long sleeve sweater. He dressed well and despite how out of place that type of outfit would look anywhere else, here he looked right at home. It dawned on me that every time I'd seen Saul, he was dressed well. I knew his attire today was his way of respecting the tournament and the game, dressed in the era of hickory shafts and knickers.

I walked up to him to say, "Hello, sir." He looked over at me. "Hey Blu, good to see ya." He paused like he was thinking of what to say next. He looked straight at me and said, "Blu, my name is Saul. I'd like you to call me that from now on. If anyone asks, tell them I told you to, but don't give them any impression that they can call me that. It's about respect, Blu, I think you understand."

"Yes sir. I mean, yes, Saul. I do, but why did you call me Blu, instead of my name?"

"Well, it was the first time I saw you," he said. "Know when that was?"

"I'm sorry, I don't," I replied. "I've seen you a number of times, but I don't recall the first time and I never thought you'd remember me."

"17th tee on number two."

"Oh," I told him, "I remember."

He went on. "I was just about to tee up my ball when I saw you. In my mind, I went back to when I was young and the first one off every day. I loved looking at the clear blue skies, framing the green of the trees. I lived for the sight of the grass on the course when everything was quiet and calm. For some reason, you brought me that feeling that day and I decided: You were going be my caddie, one day soon, and from then on. I call you Blu because of your calm and again, it's out of respect." I just nodded.

"So, from now on, when I play you are on my bag. You okay with that, Blu?"

"Yeah, that's fine with me, but one thing: Is it okay if I just call you Boss? If others hear me call by you first name, they may try to do the same and I don't think you'd like that."

He smiled and said, "I knew I was gonna like you. That's just fine, Blu." Just then, Jordon, another assistant, walked up and sat a bag next to me, holding it upright. "You might need these."

Saul looks over and says, "Blu, just set those over on the rack."

Jordan looks at me. "Blu? Is that a nickname? Where'd that come from?"

"It's out of respect," I said, pointing at Saul. Saul smiled. After Jordan walked away, I said, "You understand that everyone is gonna call me Blu, now, right? Jordon talks more than a lady at the beauty salon."

"That's okay," Saul nodded, "it fits you."

I asked if he wanted to warm up on the range. He said, "No, golf is played here," pointing at the green. Golf isn't any fun if you can't hit the ball well. What really sucks is when you give your money away to some guy because you've spent all your time beating balls and he's spent his time with a wedge and a putter. Those clubs make up half the game. If you are really good with those two clubs, it takes the pressure off the rest of the game.

Other players would come up and talk to him for a second. At first, it seemed like a kind of code or an inside joke. Soon, I realized they were making bets on today's game. I had never actually heard the terms they used before, but I was pretty sure I was right.

When we paused with no one around us, I looked at Saul and said, "Boss, can I ask you a question? If it's none my business, say so."

"Blu, you are my guy," he said. "No secrets between us. There may come a time when you ask me something that you don't want to know the answer to. So, think about that beforehand, but that being said, I'll tell you anything you want to know. As long as nothing we say goes any farther than us." He paused to look me directly in the eye. "Nothing, Blu. Okay?"

"Yes, Boss. I understand. I wouldn't want nothing different."

"Alright. Ask away, then."

"I took from what was said earlier that you're betting on today, but everyone said a number, then MM 2. What does that mean?"

"Okay," Saul said. When he said, '50 MM 2,' fifty was the amount on each bet. The M's mean Match and Medal play; two separate bets, scored differently. Match play is a hole by hole competition, each hole counting for one point. Medal play is a low total score. I know you knew that but just being clear.

"When you hear a number two after the letters, that's how many down a person is when a new bet starts. The new bet, or press, is for the same amount as the original bet, but it only lasts for the remaining holes, not the full 18. You may have any number of bets; all, except the original bet, being less than eighteen holes.

I felt stupid, struggling with simple terms I've heard all my life, but I wasn't about to interrupt him. I nodded at him and he went back to watching the putting green. I thought about what he'd just said and started putting the numbers together. He had bet over twenty guys and one girl: some hundred and five hundred-dollar bets.

Then it hit me: if someone gets hot, they could walk with twenty to thirty thousand in their pocket.

When I took another look at the tee sheet, I noticed the girl I'd mentioned earlier was in our group. As I watched her, I knew she could play. When you've been around golf as long as I have, you know if a person can play just by seeing them at a tournament. Their walk, the way they move, you can tell. I mostly noticed her because she was attractive, but she had talent. You don't see many women at these events.

Finally, about half passed 10, Saul says, "Blu, putter and three balls. please."

I got them and handed them to him. He stepped on the putting green and stopped about twenty feet from a hole. Normally Saul moved at a steady pace and never looked hurried. But now everything was crazy slow, like he was in slow motion.

He dropped the balls on the ground while I positioned myself by the hole to retrieve them after he was finished putting. Turns out that's pretty easy. You just grab them out of the cup and drop them where he points. I say 'grab them out of the cup' because he made ¾'s of them. I don't think he missed ten putts in the twenty minutes we were there. After that, he hit some chips and pitches and made some sand shots. More of the same, he made a few; all close to the hole. Finally, it was time to tee off.

I'm not going to talk about all eighteen holes here, like a buddy at the grill after a tournament that's spelling out every shot. I promise not to do that to you. Just that, on the first hole, Saul hit to the wide side of the fairway, well away from any trouble. The second shot landed on the left side of the green, about twenty-five feet away. He putted it about three feet and missed. Same on the second. From there, he hit all but one of the remaining sixteen greens. He eagled two of the par fives, birdied the other two with two putts, and made four of the other eleven birdie putts he had. He started out two over after two and shot 64 with wood shafts. Just then, I had a thought. Is it possible he bogeyed the first two holes on purpose to get a press going on all his bets?

Think about it. He is two down on all bets and has another two new bets on each match. The bets kick in when someone is two down on a bet, which was Saul was after bogeying the first two holes. This means he had four bets with each person instead of two. When he got back to even on the first bet, he would be up on both of the presses and even on the original bet. Every time he was two up on a bet, it initiated another press and the bets just kept piling up. Soon, there were six $50 bets and we were only on the fifth tee. I could see it was going to be a big day for him. It was almost hard to believe he was really that good.

After the round, he asked me to come up to the grill. Caddies don't usually eat with the players in the grill after playing, unless they are friends and not just on a day loop. It didn't surprise me at this point. In the grill, about every ten to twenty minutes, someone would come over and sit at our table, congratulate Saul, and introduce themselves to me. Most talked a bit about their round but, in the end, nobody stayed more than a few minutes and, eventually, each one handed Saul some rolled up bills, some thicker than others, and then they were off.

After the first ten players visited, Saul handed me the envelope he'd been collecting the bills in and said, "Go hand this to the head pro, nobody else. He'll be waiting." I had been paying attention and there had to be 8 to 10k in that envelope. It was one of those kinds that businesses envelopes, the big brown ones with a string to tie it shut. I did this hand off with the head pro two more times before Tania came over and sat down. She was the female in our group.

Two men from our group came over and sat down and offered small talk that was much slower and less engaging than when we first entered the grill. I guess everyone was getting tired. Both guys handed Saul a wad of cash. It was obvious these two were the whales that Saul was really here for. After those guys left, he put the money into two more envelopes. He handed one to Tania. She got up and said she'd be at home later and would be available through Thursday but had to be back for the weekend with her kids. She walked off and Saul handed me the other envelope. I got up to take it to the Pro.

"Blu, are you leaving?"

"No, sir, I'm taking this to the shop." I held the envelope up.

"Blu, that's yours for working today," he said. "You've earned it."

I undid the string and looked inside, and my jaw dropped.

Saul smiled softly. "You look like you've never been tipped well before."

I just started laughing and sat back down. Saul looked at me and said, "I know you probably want ask me a few things. Remember, I'll tell you anything, but make sure you want to know the answers. There is a big difference between thinking something is true and knowing it's true. Your perspective changes."

I was going to ask him about the first two holes, but after what he said, I decided against it. I didn't need to know. Instead I said, "Boss, when you stepped on to the putting green, till you signed your card, you moved super slowly. I noticed it wasn't jerky, like you were trying to move slowly. It was fluid, but everything you did was that way. Why is that?"

"Blu, every game has its own pace. It starts out at one speed and builds on that as other players try to go faster. That's the game they chose. But in golf, the ball is telling you to slow down to connect with it. There is an energy that connects all things that your mind wants to connect to. Once you determine what that is, then it's just a matter of calming yourself and allowing your mind to release all other thoughts. Blu, remember this, golf isn't about you making something happen. It's about getting out of your own way and allowing it to happen." He settled back into his seat. "Blu, I enjoyed today. How about you?"

"Boss," I replied, "full disclosure, these last two days have been the strangest I can remember, by far. Did I enjoy it, though?" I chuckled." Hell yes, I did, Boss."

"Good," he said. "Would you be okay working with me alone from now on?"

"Yes sir, I would."

"Okay, Blu. Here's the deal: You travel with me to matches. I will set them up, for now. Later on, you will set them up. As far as pay goes, just like today if I win, we win. If I lose, we make nothing. If you are ever in a situation where you need cash, for any reason, you just ask. When I teach, I want you there. You'll make a percentage of that, as well." He let that settle in.

"I'll see you at Pine Needles, tomorrow." said Saul. "We're going to be teaching there this year, be there at 7 a.m. Can I count on you?"

"Yes, Boss. I'll be there."

We spent that whole next day on the range. He had students stop by for lessons, but he spent most of that month teaching me. I thought of myself as a pretty good player. Someone that was knowledgeable about the swing. It took Saul all of three days to break me of that illusion. He looked at golf and the physics behind it like no one I had ever met. I learned more in those four weeks than I had in the forty years before that.

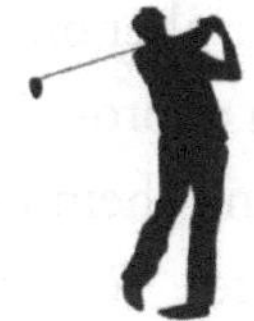

CHAPTER 3

A month or so after we met, Saul told me that we would be teaching someone for the next year, and he would be here in the morning. I got to Pine Needles just after the sun came up. The pro shop was just opening. I saw Saul sitting on a bench outside, looking out at the putting green, deep in thought. I noticed he wasn't moving a muscle, just staring. I walked up to where he was and said, "Hi boss." He motioned with his hand for me to sit on the bench with him, so I sat down.

"Blu, I wanted you here early so we could go over some things." I nodded.

"When I am teaching anyone new, from now on, you will meet with them first and take them upstairs to the grill. I need you to go over the rules with them; make sure they understand. There are no second chances, one strike and they're out. Tell them a few times so they get the importance of it. Before you meet, I will hand you a piece of paper with a number on it. That's what they will pay you in cash. If you approve of them going forward, get the money and bring them down. Okay?"

"Yes, boss," I replied. "And the rules that I go over are...?" He handed me a folded piece of paper. On one side was this:

Student Rules

1. Do not tell anyone your price to be a student of Mr. Good.
2. Do not discuss any instruction obtained from Mr. Good. You may talk about what you learned but it can never be directly linked to where they learned it.
3. Do not discuss anything observed while at this or any other establishment with Mr. Good.
4. Complete all drill assignments in the time given.
5. Never call Mr. Good by his first name. He is your instructor, not your friend.
6. Respect everything. Mr. Good, the game, and the course.

I looked at Saul and he just stared back at me. That was his way of asking if I understood.

"I got it, Boss."

Around 9 a.m., I looked over my shoulder to see what Saul was looking at. There was a man walking towards us. He's maybe six feet tall, and a well-built, good looking Italian. When he reached us, he smiled and said, "Hello." He and Saul hugged and shook hands. It was obvious that they were old friends.

Saul spoke first. "I have missed spending time with you."

The Italian nodded. "Me too, old friend."

"This is Dom Ciacchini," Saul said to Blu, his hand still on his friend's shoulder.

I gave a slight nod. "Morning, sir."

"Blu will take you upstairs to discuss a few things before we get started."

Dom nodded as I stood up. I extended my hand to shake his and said, "Sir, please call me Blu. Why don't we go upstairs to the grill to talk? Have you had breakfast?"

"I haven't and, to be honest," Dom said, "I am so excited about this that I haven't even thought about food. I guess I should eat."

As we walked away, I forgot that I was supposed to get a slip of paper with Saul's fee on it. I looked at Saul and, knowing what I was thinking, he put his hands together, curled into fists and rotated them apart, indicating I should unfold the paper. The price was on the back of the student rules. I nodded and turned back to Dom.

We walked to the grill so I could go over what I needed to say in my head. Once we were seated and the waitress had taken our orders, I said, "Mr. Ciacchini, I need to—" He stopped me.

"Blu, we are going to be spending a lot of time together over the next year. My name is Dominic. You can call me Dom. I would like to call you Blu. Is that okay with you?"

"More than fine," I told him. We went over the rules. I made sure to clearly relay to him that there would be no second chances. At some point, it became clear to me that Dom knew all of this already. This wasn't me going over the instructions. It was Dom seeing how I'm handling it all. I handed him the paper and told him to unfold it. He took it but didn't look at it.

"I know the fee I need to pay," he said. "I also know that I have to pay it before we start and that it has to be in cash."

I asked him if he could put it in an envelope. He looked at me and let out a quick laugh.

"Blu, you have no idea what this number is, do you?"

"No sir. Why?" I asked.

"I see why he trusts you. You are the perfect guy for people like Saul and me. I have a guy like you running my business, right now."

"Thank you, but what's so funny?" I wanted to know.

"You'll see. Go ask Saul for his keys to his truck."

"No need," I replied. "I have a set."

We made our way to the parking lot and he unlocked his car. He was driving a Mercedes S560. It was really something because I knew he flew in and nobody round here rents that expensive of a car. He pulled a suitcase out of his trunk, turned around and handed it to me.

"Oh." I couldn't help but feel a bit stupid. "I can see why you laughed."

I walked over to Saul's 1985 Ford Bronco and put the briefcase in the back. I had to pull back the carpet and insert the key to open the safe he had installed. I put the briefcase inside it and locked it back. I replaced the carpet, closed the door, and locked it. When I turned around, Dom was there looking at me and asked, "Aren't you going to count it?"

I said, "No." I knew the number was huge and my payday would be big, so I didn't need know now what it was in there. To be honest, at this point, I can't remember being this happy or having a friend like Saul. Plus, I was seen so differently by everyone all of a sudden. I wasn't just a caddie; I was Mr. Good's right-hand man. It was a good feeling. I wasn't about to do anything to screw it up.

We got to the practice tee and Saul was there with Dom's bag, already brought down. Saul looked at Dom.

"We got one year," Saul said. "That means we can't waste any time. If I understand this right, you need to beat Woody, who is a, what, four handicap; who may be a scratch by time the match rolls around? Unless he's stupid and underestimates you. But then again, we are talking about Woody."

Dom nodded and Saul continued.

"Every day, I'll give you one thing to do. You will need to do it enough so that, within the time period I give you, you *own* it. Can you do that?"

Dom nodded, "Yes."

"Alright," said Saul. "Let's start."

I never asked Saul about his life. Sometimes I thought he wanted me to talk more to him about it, but I was not going to be nosey. It was becoming very obvious that Dom and Saul had known each other, long before today. It's not that they acted like old friends looking to catch up, mind you. This was more like familiar business with a comfort level that made it seem almost intimate.

During the first lesson, Saul talked to Dom and had me watch and listen. He wanted me with Dom all day, every day, helping him if he got off track. Now I see why he was teaching me for the month. So, I could understand what he wanted to happen.

The next day, Saul walked up smiling, seeing that Dom had learned what he was told to, and had, seemingly, learned it well.

"Let's have lunch," Saul said to Dom.

I'm not sure if I expected to be asked to join, but I'll admit, I was disappointed that I wasn't. I stood there as they walked away, lost in my thoughts. Saul called out to me. He looked back over his shoulder and nodded his head to the side as if to say come on. I put my club in the bag and followed them up to the grill. As I walked, I felt a measure of pride. I couldn't help thinking: Wow, he wants me with him, always. Right then, I knew my life would never be the same.

At lunch, Saul asked, "Dom, what do you think?"

"Well, my left forearm is tired, kinda like in college football after a hard day in the weight room," said Dom, smiling from nostalgia.

"Well, from what I know about you, I know you always rise to the occasion."

Dom tilted his head. "Really? Thanks, Saul. It's been years since we worked together. Are you checking up on me, now?"

"Well yeah," admitted Saul. "To be honest, I had to know how hard to push you. What I heard the most was that no one could beat you from outworking you. You study more and work harder than everyone else. And if you want to know when I checked, it was yesterday. Two college teammates and your college and high school head coaches. They all said great things." Dom thought for a second then looked back at Saul.

Saul continued. "I know you well and worked closely with you, running our business. But I had to find out how to teach you. Now, I know.

Dom asked Saul, "What would have happened when I got here if you didn't get a good report from them?"

"I'm sure you would still be learning the game of golf," Saul replied. "Just not from me."

Dom smiled and looked at me, whispering, "Amazing."

"I feel like that every day," I said. "But I have a feeling by the end of the year here I may lose the ability."

I spent the next three days with Dom, going back and forth between hitting balls and watching his technique, occasionally giving my thoughts on how he was doing, if he asked. Saul stopped by a few times. At lunch, they talked about golf. Saul was always discussing the swing in abstract terms that I now understand. He spoke about the energy and, as he put it, the romance between the player, his club, and the target. He said, "The energy is there. You just have to allow the pieces to connect to one another."

He went on and on about allowing things to happen and staying out of your own way. Then, he compared it to having a child. He said, "We want to put them in a position to succeed. Just like in a swing, we put our bodies in a position to succeed, from the backswing to the top. Like children, we need to trust our swing and get out of the way – have faith that it will go well. Trust in your game. There is no room to second guess yourself.

Saul then turned to me and said, "We are going to Charlotte tonight, Blu. Do you want to come?"

"Sure."

"Be here at three o'clock and pack an overnight bag in case we stay."

I nodded.

At 3 p.m. I was talking to the attendant in the parking lot at Pine Needles. Saul and Dom pulled up in a black SUV. I got in the back and greeted them.

Dom turned to me and said, "If you need to piss, do it now. We don't stop till we get there." I nodded. "And once we're there, no one leaves until we all leave. Got it?" I nodded, again. He turned back around.

We pulled into a parking lot around 5:30p.m. It was a place called Blue Rocks, a billiard hall that was never too crowded. We walked in while Saul waited outside. Inside, Dom walked up to the bar and shook the bartender's hand, passing some bills he had folded in his grip. He said something and then nodded to a security monitor screen up in the corner. The bartender nodded and walked off. He reached under the bar and suddenly the screen went blank. Just then, Saul walked in. Dom bought us all drinks: me, a beer, Dom got a scotch and Saul, a diet cola, or pop, as he called it. Dom said he was going to warm up; that they would be coming soon. Saul said he was going to get me going on the far table. I looked at him thinking, going at what?

We walked to the table in the back that already had balls racked on it. Saul opened his case and took out his pool stick and screwed the two pieces together. He handed it to me before turning back to his case and doing the same with another two sticks. I know enough about pool to know that one was a break stick and the other he played with.

Saul broke and looked at me saying, "Blu, this is just like playing golf. First, you look at the table, you're looking for four things in the eight ball. First, what do you like stripes or solids? Once you pick, see the eight ball. Determine where you'd like to shoot it if you could now. Then look at your trouble balls, the ones that are blocked or against another ball making it a hard shot to make. Lastly, you think three shots no more. You need to think what you want to shoot first and where do you want the cue ball to be after that to make the next shot.

Saul continued. "Just like playing a golf hole. Only in golf, you think about the hole, then you play backwards, starting with where you want to hit your birdie putt from. From there, you decide what position in the fairway gives you the highest percentage chance of hitting your approach shot to that spot. Once you decide that, you select the shot you want to hit to reach the position you just selected for your approach, and where on the tee box you want to hit it from.

He told me to hit the ball around a bit thinking about what he told me and see how it goes. He turned and went to the table Dom was at and they played until a guy walked up and talked to them for a minute. Saul motioned for me to come over.

When I got to him, he introduced the guy to me and said, "We are going to play, and I need you to hold the stake and watch. Rack the balls between games. Is that ok?"

I said yes boss and racked for the first set. Saul

leaned in and whispered they were going to play one pocket.

"Watch and understand the strategy," he said. "And later we can talk about what you saw."

I nodded and watched for a while. I saw why they liked this game: it was all strategy. Saul won the first three before losing the next one, and then he won the next two.

Dom was playing a guy on the next table. It was obvious that Dom was very good at pool. I saw him run three tables in row. They were playing what I was to learn later to be 'straight' pool. It was a game played with each ball being a point with a total agreed upon prior to starting. The weird thing is you called every shot, even the break. Even stranger, when there was when only one ball left on the table, you left it as well as the cue ball. Fourteen balls were then racked with the head ball missing. The player that made the last shot continued, usually playing the ball left from the last game and breaking out the others for the next shot. It was different and interesting to watch.

When I looked at the bar, I saw I guy I knew from when I was young. His name was Kenny. He was a stocky, black guy. He grew up in the 'hood. His dad was in flooring installation and taught his sons the trade. Kenny did that, mostly, but also dealt in other activities that weren't all that on the up and up. Basically, he sold drugs and guns. He would occasionally do some "collecting" work for some people. He also would steal cars for a chop shop in Raleigh. Regardless of all that, I liked Kenny. He was fun to be with back then and nobody would fuck with him.

Once he had a guy in the neighborhood owe him money. The guy kept ducking him. Kenny put out the word that either he comes up with the cash, or he'll shoot him. One morning he sees him walking out of a Circle K. Kenny gets out of his car shoots him twice in the leg.

"You thought I was fucking with you," he says to the guy. "Pay me my money, bitch."

The guy reaches in his pocket and hands him some crunched together bills. "Here, it's all I got."

"It didn't have to be like this." Kenny sits down next to him. "Don't ever fuck me over again." Kenny sat there till the cops came and just gave himself up.

He did half of a five year sentence. When I asked him why he said, "I was nineteen, and getting punked by that bitch was just not something I was gonna let happen. Since then, nobody fucks with me. Small price to pay."

Saul took a break while the guy he was playing went to the bar. A guy I heard earlier named Rich walked up to Saul. "We need to talk, Hunter"

Saul looked at him and said, "I'm sorry but you've mistaken me someone else."

Rich started getting loud saying, "Hunter, come on, man, why are you fucking with me?"

Dom walked up straightaway and took him by the arm. He led him away from Saul behind me.

"That's Saul, you understand?" I heard him say.

Rich just looked at him as Dom continued. "If you ever want to talk with Saul privately call me. I'll set it up, but don't make no more trouble here, understand? Not here." He gave a look to Rich that was beyond intimidating. Dom went on. "Rich, you understand not to ever mention this to anyone, right? Right?" Rich nodded and Dom let him walk away.

The guy that was playing Saul had been getting beat soundly. When he came back from the bar, he was noticeably drunk and started belligerently addressing Saul, calling him a cheater. Then, he called him a stupid kike. You'd have to be pretty drunk not to notice that Saul is, by no means, Jewish. Even further, there were two Jews within ear shot that I wouldn't want to piss off.

Dom stepped in fast and, facing the guy, said, "Calm down, man. What's your name?"

"Spud," the guy said. "I go by Spud."

Okay, Spud," Dom said. "You don't have to pay my friend if you think he cheated. All I ask is that you follow your heart. Now, you live around here, right? I don't want you driving in your condition." Spud said "he was fine. This was his local spot."

Just then, a big, well-built guy, one of the Jewish guys from the far table, stepped between them and punched Spud right in the jaw, making him step back a few feet. The guy hit him again and Spud went down, hitting his head on the corner of the pool table. He was out before he hit the floor. Immediately, Dom looked at Saul and said, "We gotta go." He turned and told me to wait by the door for two minutes, no more, no less, and then to get to the car." I nodded.

He and Saul hurried out the bar. Dom looked to the bartender and held up two fingers and then three. The bartender nodded and reached under the bar. After about 2 minutes, looking at me, he pointed to the parking lot. I saw the cameras coming back up on the security screen behind him. Every frame showed, except for the parking lot. It came to me in a flash. I have one minute to be in the car and off the lot before that last camera comes up. I knew being late wasn't an option, so I ran to the car.

As I got in, Dom floored it out of the parking lot and onto the road. No one spoke as we drove, other than Saul asking if I was okay. I said I was and, after a short while, dozed off. When I woke, we were pulling up to a house. It was on a heavily wooded lot that I didn't recognize. I had no idea where we were.

We got our overnight bags and headed into the house. Dom opened the door for me. It was a large home with an open floor plan. The great room had a wall of windows on the far end, looking out at a beautiful lake. It was Baden Lake which, I knew, meant we were near the Old North State Club.

We sat and had a beer before turning in. I had a room on the second floor. Saul and Dom took suites on either end of the great room. I was out as soon as I hit the bed.

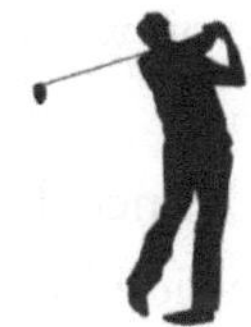

CHAPTER 4

In the morning, as I was coming downstairs, I saw Dom walking two guys to the door. The bigger of the two stopped and I could see an outline of a gun under his coat. They shook hands.

"Just have it done in a week, okay?" The guy nodded and left.

Dom turned and saw me. "Morning Blu," he said. "Let's get some breakfast." Dom led me to the kitchen where he had eggs and bacon already cooked. I poured myself some coffee and sat down to eat.

"I know Saul has talked to you, but I wanted to, as well." Dom put his hands on the table. "Whatever you see, is what you see. If you want to know something, ask me, and I'll tell you the truth. But there's two things.

One: make sure you want to know the answer before you ask. Two: never talk about anything dealing with myself or Saul. Saul is my, what's the term they use, brother from another mother." We both chuckled, and then Dom went on. "If you want out, you need to leave now."

I looked at Dom. "Since I started working with Saul, it's been a strange ride but, to be honest, I don't think I could leave, even if I wanted to. I'm learning more about everything; about golf and life. I never saw myself with this kind of life and I don't want it to end, ever. So, I'm in. I understand what that means. Just one thing, though. I don't want to be asked to do anything blatantly illegal. I'll just be here for you and Saul and on my life, I'll never talk to anyone."

Saul walked in, eating a protein bar, and asked if we were ready to go. We were, so we headed to the car and made our way to the Old North State Club. We pulled in and left our bags with the parking guy. Dom gave him the keys and slipped him what looked like a hundred-dollar bill. That was strange because he wasn't a valet just a bag guy at the bag drop to get your clubs to the pro shop . But I guess for a hundred dollars he will park your car too. We made our way to the range. It was a nice day.

We had spent just under a week there. On Saturday, we were on the range and Saul was putting, when I noticed a guy walking towards the green where Saul was. As he got closer, I saw he had a cast on his arm and his face had some scrapes on it. I soon realized it was Spud from the pool hall. I started towards Saul thinking there might be trouble, but Dom grabbed my arm. "No problem, Blu," he said. We watched as Spud walked up to Saul.

"Mr. Good," he said. "I want to apologize for the other night when I acted poorly. Also, I wanted to come and pay what I lost to you." He handed Saul some folded bills.

Spud turned and walked away. I didn't have to think twice about how Spud got roughed up or why he drove nearly two hours to pay Saul. I knew the answer whether I wanted to or not. Saul made his way over to us. When he got to where we were, he handed me a few bills that turned out to be 500 dollars.

"Here Blu," he said. "This is your share."

I put the money in my pocket and thought about how grateful I was to have someone like Saul in my life. I would work for him for free and he paid me a cut every time he made anything. I never questioned whether it was a predetermined percentage or whatever he felt like giving me. Like I said, I would have worked for free.

We spent our entire last day at the Old North State Club on the range. Saul was pleased with how Dom was progressing. Even from my point of view, it was obvious that Dom was doing great. I was certain it had everything to do with the way he went about his work. He never questioned; never complained. He just listened to what Saul had to teach him and then went at it, hard. Saul was watching Dom do a drill he'd started a few days ago and said, "This might go better than I'd expected."

Around 11:30, I saw another guy walk down towards Saul. As he got closer, I realized it was Rich, the guy from the pool hall with Kenny who had referred to Saul as Hunter. Saul noticed him and looked up. Just as Rich was about to speak, Saul went back to putting. It looked like his mind was more on what to say than on his putting. I was close enough to hear as Rich walked closer and started talking.

"Saul, please talk to me." Saul continued putting and Rich went on. "Saul, Hunter, talk to me, please." Hearing the name Hunter, Saul stopped putting and looked up. He noticed my watching and put his hand on Rich's shoulder, steering him away from me and Dom. I went to turn away and, but when I did, I saw Dom was still watching, so I stepped next to him and joined. I'm not sure of the history that Saul had with Rich, but it was obvious it had hurt Saul. At the end of the conversation, Saul put his hand to his eyes like he was wiping a tear. Then, he looked up and hugged Rich. He said something to him, then headed over to us as Rich walked back up to the parking lot. When he reached us, he looked at Dom.

"You okay, now?" Dom asked him.

"Yeah, I'm fine." Saul looked at me. "Blu get me my carry bag. Put the seven in it and bring it back down.

I am going to walk nine with Rich. You stay here and have lunch. I'll see you after."

"Are you sure, Boss?" I asked.

"Thank you, Blu, I'll be fine."

It wasn't like I thought Saul couldn't take care of himself. I just found myself being a bit protective. To be honest, I wasn't sure at the time whether I was protecting Saul or the new life he'd provided me. In the end, I decided to call it a draw.

Dom and I ate and went on working on the range. When Saul and Rich walked up from the ninth green, Saul seemed to be in much better spirits. They both smiled as they talked.

"How do you guys feel about grilling at the house tonight?" Saul asked as they approached. "Rich will be joining us."

Sure," said Dom. "I'm ready to go when you are."

Saul nodded and looked at me. "Then, let's go."

I took Saul's bag up to the shop before meeting them at the car. I rode with Dom as Rich and Saul followed us. It wasn't too long before Dom broke the silence.

"Rich was Saul's number two," he began. "And a great friend. Many believed that in a certain matter, Saul thought Rich had thrown him under the bus. at least, betrayed him, you know. I knew it wasn't true, but Saul wasn't sure. And in that type of situation, you have to be sure." He drew in a breath. "So, there you are. Now, you know what's up. Well, kind of."

"Look, I don't need to know anything," I said. "My loyalty to Saul has no conditions."

"I know," said Dom. "That's why I told you. In the last few weeks that we've gotten to know each other, I've felt certain that Saul selected the right guy."

"Selected?"

"Did you really think your being here with us was left up to chance?" Dom laughed. You worked for Eugene in Charlotte after high school. I know because I know Eugene well and gave him the money to open Terrapins". Terrapins was a pool hall in Charlotte that I worked at. I wanted to get away after losing my parents and friend within a month of graduating from high school. When you moved back home, he told me about you and wanted me to have someone to look out for you if I could. Eugene liked you a lot and worried about you when you left. Anyways, Since Saul's been here he's been keeping track of you

I just sat back and stared out the window, my mind was spinning, thinking of everything that had happened since I first met Saul. I wanted to just let it go and enjoy the ride. Mostly, because I was afraid of the answer. I remembered a movie scene with a man saying, "the most important moments in life pass you by, totally unnoticed, like a stranger in a crowd." This seemed like one of those moments. There was something about the ease in which Saul and Dom spoke with me about things. All kinds of things that, one would assume, they wouldn't want anyone to know. And then there was Dom saying that my being here wasn't by chance; that it was planned, somehow. Not that I wanted to, but what would happen if I told Saul I wanted to go back to caddying at Pinehurst? *What would happen if I didn't want this life?* Is it even an option anymore or have I unknowingly committed myself?

I wasn't sure of anything anymore.

When we got inside, Saul went out to fire up the grill and Dom went to his room to shower. I got a beer and offered one to Rich. Rich took it and, raising it slightly in the air, said, "to interesting times."

I just nodded and took a drink. Rich held his beer against his chest and looked over at me.

"So, tell me. What all do you know about everything?"

I stopped him. "Rich, anything I know, I know because Saul wanted me to. What I don't know, I don't want to know, especially from you. So, please save yourself the trouble of trying to educate me and me the trouble of having to find somewhere else to eat tonight."

I expected him to get a little pissed but, instead, he smiled. "He sure hasn't lost his touch."

I tilted my head as I tried to make sense of that. Rich went on.

"He can spot loyalty in someone like no one else, I know."

"I'll take that as a complement." I replied as I picked up the steaks from the fridge and went to join Saul.

I did not like Rich, although I could see how many people would. Looking back, I think my dislike was mostly based on jealousy of his friendship with Saul.

I gave the plate of steaks to Saul and sat down on a nearby lounge chair. After putting the steaks on the grill, he turned and leaned against the table. "How do you like Rich, Blu?"

I shook my head. "Honestly, I'm not sure. He says what he thinks, but what he says isn't everything he's thinking. I got the feeling he was interrogating me. Yeah. No, I guess, to answer your question. I don't like him."

Saul smiled. "Didn't think you would. At least, not at first."

I nodded, wondering what 'not at first' meant. Saul took a drink.

"Don't worry," he said. "You won't even have time to find out what his charm is. He's not sticking around." I guess maybe I smiled to quick or too big, but he started chuckling as he turned back to the grill. "Wow, you *really* don't like him." Saul took another swig of his beer and Rich came walking out towards the grill.

"What are you guys talking about?" said Rich, looking at Saul.

"Loyalty." Saul said, making Rich smile. "There's an important subject."

Saul quickly followed up. "Yes, in practice as well as appearance." Rich's smile faded.

"Yes, it is, Saul."

Dom walked out saying, "Are we eating or am I setting up a boxing ring." Everyone chuckled and we went to the table to eat. I felt, right then, that Rich would never be a permanent fixture in our group, and I was glad. He talked and thought in puzzles, always trying to work an angle. He was a real smart guy, but you wouldn't know it from how he looked; tatted and grungy.

I grew up with a guy like that. He was a sociopath and it took me twenty-five years to figure that out. Rich was the exact opposite in personality and looks, both the physical and projected, but there were also similarities, at the same time. I did not like this guy. It was like I already had history with him, bad history. Anyway, he left that evening and I didn't see him again for a while. Saul, Dom, and I finished our beers and went to bed.

The next day, Saul dropped me off at my place. "Tomorrow, when you get to CCNC, tell them my name at the gate. We will be there through the Fall." I knew why. CCNC was a gated community and I knew why people like Saul lived there. He never *had* to leave the gates if he didn't want to. No one could make him. And after Charlotte, I did not think he wanted to leave those gates.

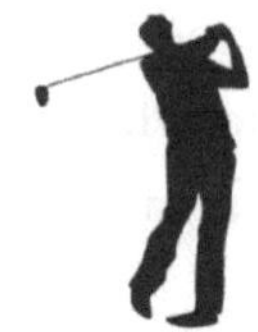

CHAPTER 5

We had breakfast together at the club. Not long after we sat down; Saul spoke up.

"I have this friend," he began. "I taught him a few years ago. He's on the Web.com Tour, now, and needs a caddie for a few weeks. He called and asked if I knew anyone and I told him I did. I would like you to help him for the next month. Is that alright with you?"

"Whatever you need, Boss," I agreed.

The next day, I drove down to South Carolina; Greer, more specifically. I got a loop on the Web.com Tour with a player named Ben Baits from Georgia. He was a good player, from what I'd read about him. I was going to be on his bag for two weeks in the south, then off for one week, then back with him in western New York.

During the break, I would be home with Saul for one week then up to NY with Ben. The first two weeks went well. We made checks and he was doing pretty well for the season. To be honest, I liked Ben. He was a real southerner with a comforting drawl. He wasn't a kid anymore and actually had some sense about him. He went about his work with a seriousness that I appreciated in a player. At any other time in my life, I would just stay right here and ride his bag to the tour. However, I found myself missing home and working for Saul.

When I got back, after those two weeks, I got a message from Saul to meet him at the club in the morning. When I got to the Pro Shop, Dom and Saul were eating breakfast in the grill. I pulled out a chair and joined them.

"How'd it go with Ben?" Saul asked.

I told him what I thought. "He is a good player and made some good checks," I said, "but I miss working here. I like being home." I asked, "This isn't your way of getting rid of me, is it Boss?" I tried to make my smile look less forced than it was. Truthfully, I needed to know, though I'm not exactly sure I wanted to.

"You're my guy, Blu. That's not gonna change," said Saul. "I just need you to do this for two more weeks. I need you to go to New York and caddie for him there. You will leave a week early and play the Peak'n Peek course a few times, just to get a feel for it. Keep your phone with you and accept any invitations you get to play elsewhere." He took a sip of his drink. "Now, the important part, Blu. Do you remember our rule?"

"We have a few," I replied. "Are you talking about never speaking about our time together?"

Saul leaned in over the table.

"Yes," he said. "Further than that, never mention me or Dom to anyone. If somehow you are asked: you have no idea who we are." He leaned back in his chair. "That alright with you, Blu?"

I told him it was fine. "Whatever you say, Boss, I mean, *sir*." I extended my hand. "My name is Blaise. I don't think we've met before."

Saul and Dom laughed. Saul shook my hand saying, "Hi, Blaise. I'm Mr. Cooper. B.D. Cooper."

"That won't send up any red flags, huh?" Saul shook his head. We were still smiling when we got up from the table and headed to the range.

The view of the course was beautiful. Everything was green; morning dew still sat on the fresh cut grass. I looked at Saul as he turned his head to me. I nodded towards the course. "It's beautiful." He smiled again.

"Yes, Blu. It sure is."

Dom was smiling, listening to us. "Guys, I really had no idea before I came here why you get all misty eyed about this game. I do, now. Working at your game lets you see the real beauty it offers. How many times must I have walked past the course at my home club and not noticed? It's a funny thought; I have Woody to thank for all this. I need to do that. Yeah, right after I kick his ass in our match."

It was nice to hear Dom say that. He was learning a lot and working hard. To be honest, I was amazed at his progress. He was happy with it, too, and kept mentioning how amazing the game was. I knew then that he would play golf forever. It's that feeling when the game touches your soul, when you know you've found what you've been searching for. It's like a home that you never knew existed. Saul mentioned before that until it touches your soul you can never be really good at the game.

Saul asked me if I was packed, and I told him I was. "Good," he said. "While Dom is working on the range, I want to go over your thoughts on your last two weeks with Ben.

When we finished, Dom showed up and tossed me his keys. He told me to take his car up to NY. He said that he would be with Saul the whole time and, as I have a long drive ahead of me, I should go in style. He said he may want me to leave it there and if so, he would line up a car for me to drive back. I didn't ask for details. I had learned not to.

The next morning, I was off to Clymer, NY. Dom's car was a big boy Mercedes and rode like a magic carpet. I loved it. I was driving through West Virginia when my mind went back to when I was younger with that guy, Kenny, from the pool hall. He told me a story I hadn't thought about in years. It made me laugh because it truly summed up Kenny's whole M.O.

He told me he was up in Virginia with his brother and his family. They were visiting for Easter and sometime during the visit he got into it with his sister-in-law. It seems the name calling got so bad that she told him there was no way in hell he was riding back with them to Charlotte. So, he calls a cab to go to the bar and an idea comes to him.

He was all dressed up for this family thing and had the cab driver to drop him off at a country club where his father had worked when he was younger. He told Kenny all about the place and they had driven by it many times on family get-togethers.

Not having a ride home, Kenny thought he might be able to procure a car from some, as he put it, *fat-ass rich cracker*. While walking up the entrance, he took off his coat and stopped right by the front door. He said it wasn't five minutes before *some fat motherfucker* pulls up and hands him the keys, along with a twenty-dollar bill. He said, "Thank you, sir. Enjoy your day, sir," and jumped in the car.

I asked him, "What would've happened if you got caught."

"Caught doing what?" he replied.

"Stealing a car from a fat guy at a golf club."

"I didn't steal it," he said, "he gave it to me." So, I asked him what he'd say if they asked him what he was doing there? He tells me, "I'd say that I was applying for a job."

"Okay, then did you apply?" I mocked.

"No," he said, "I needed the job to buy a car, and that guy just gave me one, so I didn't need the job anymore."

I still chuckle again all these years later, just remembering that story. He said that man's car was at a shop in Raleigh, chopped up, before the poor guy got off the ninth green.

I checked into my hotel late that afternoon. After getting situated, I headed to the course we would be playing for the next week. I spoke with one of the assistants and he gave me a tee time, early the next morning. I was paired with one other guy whose name I did not recognize. It seemed as if, the whole time, I had been waiting for something strange to happen, but nothing out of the ordinary ever went down. I'm not sure how that made me feel. Maybe relieved, but a little disappointed, too.

I realized that I was growing an addiction to this new life. It was like a dream that I didn't want to wake up from. Not only was it exciting, but from working with Dom and Saul, my game had gotten good. Damn good. I thought I was a pretty good amateur player before. Suddenly, I was well beyond that. I was shooting under par just about every time I played. The weird thing was, I expected to. That's one feeling I never thought I would experience.

The next morning, I was up early for a 7:20 tee time. I arrived at the course and hit four or five golf balls; a few putts before going to the first tee. The Starter and I talked for a few minutes till a man came walking up to us. The Starter looked up and said, "Mr. Kell, this is Mr. Jones." He gestured at me. "He's playing with you, today."

I extended my hand and said, "You can call me Blu."

"Hi, Blu," he said. "I'm Mike." He pointed at the tee. "Why you don't lead us off?"

Mike was a pretty good player. He was maybe fifty years old, bald on top, around Saul's age. He looked kind of like Tony from The Sopranos. We talked for a bit and he told me he was from Erie, Pennsylvania. His father played on the Tour for a few years they were both members at Kahkwa Club. I had heard of that course before, but I couldn't remember where. I found out later from Mike that they had the U.S. Women's Open there in 1970. That was probably why knew of it.

During the round, I hit putts from several spots to where I thought the pins might be placed during next week's tournament. I didn't make take any notes, just tried to get a feel for the greens. I did make notes of the large slopes on the greens, though. That might be important.

I liked Mike. He was easy to talk to, even though I avoided some subjects. I mainly talked about caddying for Ben and what it was like. I spoke in broad terms, allowing him to think I caddied on tour for much longer that I did. I stretched my experience on the course from a few weeks into a few years. You know, never lying, but letting him make his own assumptions along the baselines of what I had said. And on some of what I didn't say, too. Sometimes you have to do that sort of thing. It occurred to me that I was getting pretty good at being elusive. I guess Saul had rubbed off on me.

After the round, Mike and I had lunch and he asked me to join him again for a round the next morning. I accepted. I was curious as to why he wanted to play with me again but didn't think about it much.

The next day went similarly to the day before with friendly conversation and good golf. He ended up shooting a 69, which was good for this course. We parted as friends and afterwards I went to the range for about an hour. The Head Pro came up and we talked a bit.

I got a golf cart around 4 in the afternoon and went out to map the greens for Ben. I made notes of the landing area for each possible pin position and targets on the green from different angles. I did this for the next two days, mapping six holes a day.

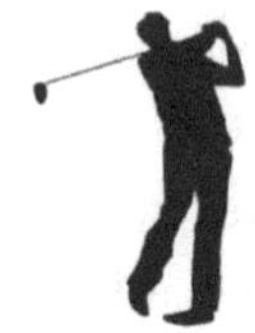

CHAPTER 6

Thursday, I got a call from Mike. He invited me to play with him at his club that afternoon. He said he needed a partner in a match and wanted me. Since most of my work for Ben was finished, I agreed. I packed a bag and headed for Kahkwa Club.

The entrance was lined with oak trees that formed a canopy about twenty-five feet above the ground. It made you feel like you were driving through a green tunnel with daylight only coming through from the other end. I wondered if this is what near death experiences are like. Go towards the light and come out on the other side, reborn. As I got to the end of the trees, I saw a huge English Tutor clubhouse surrounded by the same towering oak trees. It was breathtaking and it reeked of money.

About an hour before our tee time, I went to the pro shop and they directed me to the driving range where I was to meet Mike. We hit balls for a bit, then a man walked up to Mike and asked him if he was ready to get his ass kicked.

"No. I thought we were playing you and Capote," he replied. "I wasn't aware we changed matches." He and Mike both laughed.

Mike introduced me. "Blu, I'd like you to meet Woody." As I shook his hand, everything started to make sense now. This was why I was here.

"So, you're the ringer he brought in, huh?" Woody said.

"I don't know about that," I replied. "I'm just a caddie. The only way I get close to real good golf is with a bag on my shoulder."

"Why don't I believe that?" Woody asked with a smile.

He introduced me to a guy named Mike Capote, we shook hands. He was a lefty who looked like he could play. Not a great swing, but his shots all had the same shape, nothing off line. I remembered something Saul once told me, "Don't be looking at the guys on the range with great swings. They may be good, or they may not be. If you see a guy with an okay swing or a bad one, even, look out. He's here for a reason. Most likely, it's because he's got a great short game. If he hits it well that day, he could shoot nothing."

We teed off around 2p.m. I noticed there were not many golfers on the course. A few early morning tee times were finishing up, but other than that, it was empty. Mike made bets on the first tee and I realized, true to form, we were playing for money. A lot of money. They decided to play ten-dollar Vegas.

The rules were pretty simple: put you and your partner's score on each hole together, lowest score first. Compare them to your opponent's number and the difference is what the team with the lowest number gets at ten bucks a point. This is where it can get expensive. If both players are over par, you use the high number first.

So, if your partner makes an eight and you lip out for par, a 48 goes to 85 on the lip out. Here is another piece to the game: a team down can press a bet at any time. A press doubles the stakes, so with the first press, a bet of $10 per point goes to $20 per point, and on the second press, $20 goes to $40. So, you can see how this could get out of hand, financially.

After the bets were made, their team hit first. Capote teed up his ball. Mike stood next to me and leaned in. "Don't worry about the bet, Blu, I got us covered. Just play golf." I nodded.

The first hole was a straight away par four. Mike hit it, stiff, and made birdie. I went, two putts for par. On the second hole, we are up, and they press the bet, making it $20 a point. Mike hits a good drive, eighty yards from the hole, so I step on it a bit. This a short hole and would be drivable *if* you kill it. The landing area slopes left to a high rough and there's a flat area, ten yards wide, on the right side.

My ball landed on the flat and rolled onto the front of the green. Woody hit a hybrid, a hundred yards out. Capote hit with his driver, dropping it perfectly onto the landing area, but the ball kicked right and found the rough on the right side of the green, 10 yards short. We were all on, with Woody closest in two at about five feet. I was putting for an eagle, from about 30 feet, with a large right to left break. I rolled my putt to a foot away. Both Mikes missed. That left Woody and I; if we both make; we tie the hole.

He hit the right lip of the hole and it spun out. Woody rushed his putt instead of taking his time. It was like he wanted it over. He did not seem at all comfortable with the pressure. They conceded my putt, so we won another 10 points, or $200, on that hole.

On the next tee, another press. Mike smiled and winked at me. He wasn't at all worried about the money or the stakes we were getting to. I knew that, with the last press, we were at $40 a point. If it were my money, I'd be nervous. But Mike? Not so much.

The round went on to the 8th tee. It was a shortish par five, dogleg right, and it was there that we ran into another group that was taking their time on the course, playing it slowly. Suddenly, Mike spoke up saying that he saw a two on this hole once. "You know Hunter, pointing at Capote, "he hit a 4 iron from dead center in the fairway, two hops and then in."

Capotis spoke up, "Hunter? Whatever happened to him? He played every tournament in sight and then he was gone."

"You were his friend. Do you know?" "Capote said to Kell. "Yes and no. His mother died and he did not take it well. I saw him a few times, around then. He was kind of fucked up about it. He started playing pool and drinking; doing too much of both."

"You know," Woody chimed in. "I saw him a few times out playing pool. He could play and he hung with some pretty shady-looking guys. Seemed like a lot of money was on the line each time I saw him. What did he do for a living anyway?"

"I got no clue," said Capote. He looked at Mike Kell. "Didn't you caddie for him in the classic?"

"Yea I did," said Kell. "That was the year Trevino and Chip Beck had a playoff. Couldn't tell you who won, but he could have gone low in that one. He was five under on the 14th hole, a par five, with an iron into the green in two. He hits it just over the back. He didn't get up and down, so he makes par, then misses his short birdie putts on the next two holes. 17th hole, he hits a drive right down the center.

The ball hits a sprinkler head and kicks dead right, under a tree. It was maybe the second most amazing thing I've seen with him. He shoots 68 that round and finishes 5th or 6th." He paused. "But to answer your question, no, I have no idea what he did for a living. He was with Dominic a lot. Why don't you ask him?"

Everyone laughed. I faked it.

"No thanks," said Capote, "I'm addicted to living." That's when he looked at Woody and said, "That's right, you and Dom got a match coming up, don't ya?"

Woody nodded. "Fuck him." he said.

"What is it with you two, man?" Capote asked. "You were buddies once. What the fuck happened?"

Woody just shook his head. "Ask Dom."

It was time to hit our drives. Woody was visibly upset; pissed off by the conversation. I killed a drive down the right tree line with a hard draw and it ended up on the left side of the fairway. Kell hit a fade in the middle, maybe twenty yards behind mine. When Capote got up to hit, he left it short in the left center of the fairway. He didn't hit it very well, but it stayed in play with a long way to the green.

Now Woody, still pissed, pulled it way left and out of bounds. He hit it again; did the same thing only shorter and in play, but just barely. He slammed his driver into the ground. "Fuck you!" he screamed at no one in particular.

We got to our shots and Woody needed to punch out into the fairway. Capote was a long way from the green, but theoretically could get there, so we found ourselves waiting again. I was standing with Capote and Kell, with Woody way back by his ball. Kell looked at Capote.

"Wow, aren't you glad you brought Dom up to your partner?" We all chuckled.

"Whatever it is between them, it's something big," said Capote. "I've never seen Woody like that, ever. No more talking about Dom."

"Are you kidding?" Kell laughed. "That's all I am talking about this whole round. I may retire early."

"I swear to God," said Capotis. "If you say anything before this round is over…" He was serious now, looking right at Keim.

"I know. I'm just fucking with you," Kell says.

The group in front was off the green, so we went to hit. Capote hit fairway wood and striped it at the left side. As it flew, Capote started yelling at the ball, "Get up, get up!" It looked good but was close to not clearing the trap. He yelled again, "Get up!" The ball fell short. It looked like it hit the face of the bunker and stayed.

As Kell walked up to his ball, it occurred to me: if Capote doesn't make par, this could be a huge hole for us. Kell hit a hybrid that lands on the left-center of the green, but with a back right pin position, he was still maybe forty feet away. It was my turn and I pulled out a 4 iron after figuring the yardage to the back edge of the green. With a 4 iron, I knew I couldn't hit it over, so I just swung smoothly and hit a high draw, tracking the pin. When it landed, it took a small hop and stopped. It looked close, real close.

When we got to the green, things did not go well for them. Capote had plugged it in the lip of the trap. He could swing at it, but all he could do is have it roll back into the center of the trap. Woody chunked it into the left trap and barely got out of it onto the front fringe lying six. Capote, now hitting four, hit it maybe fifteen feet short of the pin. We got on the green and, true to form, Woody 2 putted for 8 and Kell follows suit by putting twice for 4.

Capote hit his putt and it looked good from the time it left his putter. Three feet from the hole, it hit a ball mark that made it hop. Not a lot, but enough. His ball hit the left lip, circled around, and came back to the front of the hole. It was lying on the front edge of the cup. It looked like it would fall, but it just sat there. He took his time walking to it, hoping it would slip in. A gust of wind came up and he stopped, waiting to see if it was enough to push it over the edge. Finally, he tapped it in and, louder than normal, said, "Fuck you, ball!"

It's my turn and I think back to something Saul taught me:

> *Clear your mind, read the putt, pick a target, and hit it. Nothing else matters. Whether it goes in or not has nothing to do with you. All you can do is hit it at the target.*

I went through my steps and picked a spot, two

inches outside of the hole. I lined everything up, looking down the line twice, and stroked the putt, dead center. Kell let out a, "That's my partner!" The bet was $80 per point and they went 86 to our 34. That's a $4,000 hole. These guys got serious in a hurry.

The match went back and forth until we hit #18. This hole was a straight away par four; no traps, just green and, man, was it green. The fairway ran up hill in the landing area then back down slightly. Fifty yards from the green, it sloped back up to the front edge. The green was domed a bit and fell from back to front. It was surrounded by pine trees and above the trees was the bluest sky. The colors were so vivid, they seemed almost pastel. I thought back to my time with Saul, sitting on the bench at Pine Needles in the morning.

Saul talked often about the calm that drew him to an early morning course. It had a beauty that touched his soul whenever he saw it. I felt exactly what he had described looking out from the tee, now. The feeling seemed to elevate me and peel away any other thought other than where I was now. It felt incredible, almost spiritual. The quiet was deafening and my skin had an electricity to it that resonated from within my muscles. It must be what heaven feels like.

Looking back, I realized that I was somewhere I never wanted to leave. I would have thought that at the time, but I had no concept of time. I know it sounds cliché, but I was solely in that moment. I wasn't thinking about staying or leaving. I also realized, in that daze, that I had no fears or expectations. That's what's really stuck with me: an utter void of expectations.

"Blu, you gonna hit?" Kell's words brought me back from my daydreaming.

I teed up and approached the ball. My movements were slow. There was no hurry and I knew what I wanted to do with this shot. I had no thoughts other than hitting, exactly as my mind saw it. It was the most natural thing I could do and not hitting the shot was simply unfathomable. I felt like crying tears of joy and thanking God for bringing me to that point.

As I expected, I hit my drive down the right-hand side, drawing back to the center and coming to rest just over the ridge in the fairway. I would like to tell you where everyone hit their drives on that hole, but I had no idea. I was barely aware that anyone else existed. I strolled, almost floated, up the fairway some thirty yards behind my playing partners.

The others had hit by the time I got to my shot. All three were on the green with one ball close, about four feet behind the hole. From the position of the ball mark, I realized it was Woody who hit it. That thought did nothing to change my focus. I determined where I wanted to hit my putt from. I saw the shot I wanted to hit. I approached the ball. Then suddenly, I saw it flying against the blue sky.

I don't have any memory of swinging the club or even moving my body. I was just standing there in the finish position. My body weight was perfectly balanced over my feet which were firmly anchored to the ground. The ball seemed to hang in the air forever, finally passing through the dark green of the trees. It slipped, a crescent of white, behind the trees and then onto the bright green of the grass surrounding the hole. It bounced softly and rolled forward, right to where I wanted it: ten feet short of the hole. That left me headed uphill with a slight right to left break.

The other two had twenty-foot putts on the green and both missed, tapping in for par. I lined up my putt; one cup, outside right. I picked the spot I wanted to start it on and stroked it, dead center. Woody took a first, then a second walk around the hole, looking at his putt. His line was downhill, and six inches left of the hole. I looked at Woody and recognized the look on his face.

Like a wave hitting me, I knew exactly what that look was about. More than that, I understood it. My mind went to a place that I didn't know existed before this, like a secret room full of enlightenment. Just pick a subject and imagine being given full understanding of it all.

Right now, I understood. Woody had a hundred thoughts going through his head, but only one emotion.

Fear.

I was aware it existed, like the trees behind the green, but it was of no matter to me at that moment. I saw it on Woody's face.

Woody was doing his best to push it down, to deny

its existence, but by doing so, it only grew. It fed off the doubts in his head, getting bigger and bigger. As it grew, more thoughts appeared, more doubts. It was all food to the beast growing inside his mind. I knew, at that moment, the only chance he had of making his putt was luck. Don't get me wrong, I enjoy being lucky as much as anyone else, but I couldn't imagine it being my only hope in life.

He missed the cup by two inches and the ball rolled five feet passed. Honest to God, it was the worst fucking putt I have ever seen. It was so bad, the other two just broke out into laughter. Woody gave them the finger, walked up, and hit his next putt into the hole, without thinking, exactly as he should have done on the first try.

This is what Saul has been teaching me the whole time, leading me to this place. I realized, awareness is not genetic, but it's available to everyone. You just have to let go and allow it to invite you in.

I heard Saul's words in my head:

> *Golf isn't something you do. Once you have the skills in place, it's something you allow to happen. Just get out of the way. Golf is a romance. It's the love of your life. That's how it's to be treated. It will treat you the same. It's a place, void of violence. It's a slow dance. It's beautiful.*

We made our way to the grill room after the drinks

arrived and we'd settled our bets. Woody handed me a roll of bills, saying, "Nice round, Blu." I unrolled them and noticed there were $500 bills in the roll. Who carries $500 bills around? These guys are whales.

"That was a nice round of golf, Blu." Kell said after the waitress left with our food orders.

I thanked him, realizing that I hadn't even thought about what my score was. I had finally crossed the threshold to where I was able to separate shots from each other in my mind. I only focused on the task at hand: the next shot. I had been able to do that for short periods of time, for a few shots or for a couple of holes. But that was as far as I could maintain that mind set. Without realizing it, I had just done it for the first time, today, for an entire round of golf. I reached for the card. A 68. I shot a 68 today.

The guys were shooting the shit about the round when Keim cleared his throat to get everyone's attention. "You know we were talking about Hunter and all," he said, "and it made me think of something else. You guys know my wife's a realtor, right? She listed his house a couple of years back. He contacted her by email asking her to list it. He told her where the key was and when she went to look it over, it was still full of stuff. Not just furniture, I mean, clothes in the closet and dresser, tools; everything was still there."

"I asked her if there were any golf clubs or golf stuff, but there weren't. I know he had a lot of clubs, hundreds, and books back to the 1800s. They were all gone. When she emailed him back asking about it, he told her to sell it all and to keep the money for doing it. She asked if he was sure and his response just said: S'all good."

"So, the house sells for the likes of five hundred grand and he's set up an account for it. He had the firm that handled the closing manage it till he contacts them. Well, last month I had a meeting with the president of the company, and he asked me about Hunter. It seems the money's still there. I asked if he could be dead. The president said he gets emails now and again saying that he will be in touch soon with where to send the money. As of last month, nothing has stated where, yet."

"He was a strange guy, always in a hurry," Capote said. "Talked to himself constantly; hyper as shit when he wasn't on the golf course. He was a different person on the course. He was pretty good, too. Then, he started working on his game with Bobby in Pittsburg. In one summer, he changed everything: his swing and, especially, his short game. After that summer, he had a short game that was so good it seemed like all he did when he practiced was wedges and putting. You asked about what he did for a living. Well, I'm pretty sure he was connected. I know Dom is and I am certain they worked together."

"Here's another crazy thing about him," said Kell. "He got shot in Charlotte, you know. Yeah, it was a quite a few years back, leaving a bar where he played pool. It was Christmas Eve. I know because, even though he had a brother in Charlotte, he had me as his emergency contact. I hadn't talked to him in years when I got that call. I called his brother and, three days later, went down to see him in the hospital. He was gone."

"When I talked with the doctor that operated on him, she told me he had flat lined, twice. She said he should still be in the hospital and would have needed to stay another three weeks before being released. I guess a private ambulance service came in and took him away. She had no idea to where. I tried calling him at the number I had, but it wasn't in service anymore. I sent him an email and he responded the next day. All it said was: Thanks, Mike. S'all good. I haven't heard from him since."

"Yes sir, now I am sure he worked with Dominic," said Woody. "Probably became a douche bag, too."

"What is this thing with you and Dom," Capote looked at Woody, "you have got to let it go."

Woody just shook his head. "I'll let it go when that fucker is dead."

The mood was broken, and a silence fell over everyone. Kell stood up. "Blu, you ready? I gotta get home. You can stay at my place tonight." I stood, too, and thanked the other guys for the match. I went to Mike's, then got up early the next morning and went back to The Peek to get ready to meet Ben. will bury you, himself. Then, when on Saturday.

Hole	1	2	3	4	5	6	7	8	9	10	11	12	13	14	15	16	17	18	Total
Players																			
Team 1																			
Blu	4	3	3	4	3	4	3	3	4	4	3	5	4	5	3	4	4	3	
Mike Kim	3	4	3	5	4	4	5	4	4	4	2	4	4	6	3	4	4	4	
Team one hole (total score)	34	34	33	45	34	44	35	34	44	44	32	45	44	56	33	44	44	34	
Team 2																			
Capote	4	4	3	4	3	4	3	6	4	4	3	4	4	5	3	4	4	4	
Woody	4	4	3	5	4	5	4	8	4	4	2	5	4	6	3	4	4	4	
Team one hole (total score)	44	44	33	45	34	45	34	86	44	44	32	45	44	56	33	44	44	44	
Bet by hole — Team 1	10	10	-	-	-	-	-1	52	-	-	-	-	-	-	-	-	-	10	
Press		*	*				*	*											
Per point	$10	$20	$40	$40	$40	$40	$40	$80	$80	$80	$30	$80	$80	$80	$80	$80	$80	$80	
Bet Running total — Team 1	10	30	30	30	30	30	28	300	300	300	300	300	300	300	300	300	300	380	x $10 / point
																			$3800/man

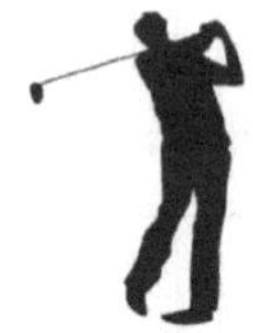

CHAPTER 7

The tournament was a lot of fun. Being around that many good players is an experience that, if you've never had it before, would be lost on you. Sure, there are good players at every club that play golf together. They think they have a good handle on what good golf really is. They also believe they're close to playing at the next level. Truth be told, they aren't even close. There are a hundred plus tour-caliber players that all spend every waking moment working towards the same goal of playing on the PGA tour. The entire mind set is different. The way they talk and how they share with each other is so unlike normal experiences with real players.

Being around one or a few players at this caliber

was different, also. Usually, in club settings or in small groups, these players kept to themselves and didn't really share with regular golfers the true insights that they had. It wasn't meant to be rude; it was just that they knew regular players wouldn't understand. It's like the "you had to be there" syndrome. And being there, it was magical. They all shared openly on a totally different level. I can't really explain it any better than that.

It had been so long since I had caddied in a tour event that I'd forgotten what it was like. At the end of it all, I was really glad I came. Ben finished fifth, made a good check and paid me well.

That was another thing that really stuck out in my mind. Ben didn't do anything amazing. As a matter of fact, a lot of other players were much more impressive, but Ben had a way of playing a course that left nothing to chance. Every day, he hit fifteen to seventeen greens, always hitting it well away from trouble. And he never chased a pin that was difficult or tucked in a corner. He'd be a boring 18 under for the tournament and, unless you paid attention, you would have no idea he was under par at all.

I could tell he'd worked with Saul before just from watching him play. Saul's words played in my head all four days I was there:

> *Hit 16 greens and be a great player with your wedge and putter.*

Another thing I noticed was that there were some players that would tell you how things are, either with the golf swing, short game, or how to play the course we were at. Those guys, even though they acted like they knew everything, were actually scared. They didn't want to let doubt into their thoughts and, in turn, they aren't getting better. Then there were those, like Ben, who listened to everyone and actually wanted to share their thoughts. I soon looked at him as a true student of the game. I asked him about it, and he said, "This is a journey, being out here, and nowhere else can you learn to play golf like being here. I want to learn all I can because one day it will end. I don't want any regrets." I liked Ben a lot. He was kind and dealt with a lot of the egos out there with a lot of tact. Plus, the fact that he had been playing so long he was well respected by most everyone there.

On the last day of the tournament, I saw these two guys that looked out of place. They were in dress pants and short sleeve bowling shirts with dress shoes, not golf shoes or sneakers. It was before the round and they seemed to be paying close attention to Ben as he warmed up. First on the range and then on the putting green. I didn't think much of it and quickly put it out of my mind.

I saw them at the turn and again when we finished up. I was tending to Ben's clubs as he went to the scorer's tent. When he exited the tent, the two men appeared and talked with him. I was close enough to hear. They asked if he knew a guy and raised a picture up for Ben to look at. He said, "Yes, I knew him well. Why do you ask?" They said they were trying to find him, and Ben told said, "Good luck. He died about ten years ago." They asked if he was sure about that and Ben said, "I went his funeral. Yeah, I'm pretty sure." With that, he brushed past them and approached me, asking me to follow him to put his clubs in his car.

I asked, "What was that all about."

He told me "I don't know just some guys chasing a ghost, I guess. Nothing I like to think about though." I noticed he was upset by their questions, but I didn't inquire any further. Whatever it was, it made him sad, just thinking about it.

In the parking lot, as I was leaving, I saw the two guys get in a car and exit behind me. I spotted them again on I-79 South in West Virginia and on 77 South in Virginia. I thought it was just because it was the main roads south and we were on the same path, heading from the tournament to the south east. I didn't see them again and focused on getting home. I enjoyed caddying for Ben, but I was eager to get back to my life.

The drive back to CCNC was long. I got in late Sunday night. I enjoyed that the trip, but I missed being home. Honestly, I missed being with Dom and Saul. I kept having this fear that my new life would somehow come to an end and I would be filled with dread. I haven't been asked to do anything that I wasn't more than willing to do; nothing that was illegal or dangerous. That being said, it felt like I was waiting for the other shoe to drop.

I got up early the next morning and headed to the clubhouse to meet with Saul and Dom for breakfast. When I got there, they were already sitting in the grill. I sat down and Dom immediately started talking to Saul. "Were going to have a visitor today."

Saul asked who.

"Steve," Dom answered, "the teacher called me few days ago and said he needed to talk to me. He wouldn't say anything over the phone. You may want to be here. ." Pointing to Saul "Whatever it is it concerns you"

"What are you thinking?" Saul asked.

"Well, said Dom. "I have a feeling it has to do with Vincent. And if so, we have to handle it."

"Listen," said Saul. "Steve is good man. He may the best person I have ever known. He is big-time Christian and you can't get him caught up in anything. I'll do whatever to protect him and his family. Whatever it takes." Saul paused. "Is that good with you?"

Dom scratched his ear. "Look, I've only met him a few times through those tournaments you talked me into sponsoring, and I liked him. So, yeah, that's good. Let's wait and see how serious this really is, okay? He's gonna be here around ten."

We ate and went to the range to warm up. Right at ten, a man walked over to us. He was a thin man with white hair. He had a smile that everyone caught when they saw it. He was dressed like a well-dressed golf pro would be dressed. He shook hands with Dom, and then with Saul. They looked at each for a moment while holding their handshake and then they hugged.

When they finished, Steve said, "I thought you would be skinnier." Dom laughed out loud. It seemed like Saul was close to tears, but that turned to a smile when he heard what Steve said. I didn't get it.

"Steve, I've missed you," said Saul. "I'm sorry about any trouble I may have caused you."

"Don't worry," Steve replied. "It's alright. But we do need to talk."

"Let's go to my house instead of here," Saul replied. They agreed and then suddenly Saul stopped and turned to me. "Blu, I want you meet Steve Bosh." We shook hands, exchanging hellos. "Blu, this is one of my oldest friends. Would you like to join us?"

I looked at Dom then Steve. They looked at me, straight faced, and I couldn't get a read from their expressions whether they wanted me to come or not. I decided to reply with, "If you want me with you, Boss, I'll go." He nodded that he did and off we went. We got to Saul's house and sat on the patio. Steve started telling Dom about the reason he came.

"Dom, I had a student that bought three months of golf lessons from me. His name is Paul Cicero." Steve paused as he noticed that Dom smiled when he heard the name. "What, you know him?"

"No," said Dom. "Go on. I'll tell you later." Steve continued.

"He took his first lesson and it went well for about thirty minutes. Then he started asking about you." He pointed at Saul. "He was masking it with normal talk, reminiscing about his college days and asking about mine. But when I tried to change the subject, he just kept on, then turned it to asking about you directly and the last time I saw you," pointing at Saul. "I felt like I was being interrogated. What bothers me the most is that he's a scary guy." Steve turned to Dom. "I knew you two were close, so I wanted to talk to you about it."

"But I didn't expect to see *you*," focusing his attention back on Saul. "Last I heard, you *died*." I chuckled and everyone turned to look at me. "Skinnier," I said with sarcasm.

Dom smiled. "Finally got it, huh?" Dom, turned back to Steve and asked, "So, what did you tell him?"

"I told him the truth. As I knew it, at least. The last time I saw you," he said to Saul, "was eleven years ago, about six months before your funeral. We talked, two years before that, about personal things and your faith. I told him I was counseling you. That's all I knew to say."

He looked at Saul, then at Dom, then down at his hands, clasped tightly together on the table in front of him. "Listen, I don't mean to offend anyone. I never asked what either of you do for a living and I don't care to know. I make no moral judgment on either of you, that's not my place. That being said, I'm not stupid." He paused again to think of what to say next. "I mean this respectfully. My son teaches with me and my wife works at the school. I can't have this at our club or anywhere near my family. I was going to refer him to another teacher nearby but, honestly, I'm scared of this guy. He's just…evil. So, there you have it."

Dom sat back in his chair and stroked his chin. He sat forward again to look at Steve before saying, "Okay. I understand. When's his next lesson?"

"Thursday at eleven o'clock."

"Keep that lesson," said Dom, "and I'll ask a friend to go up and afterwards have a talk with him; get him to realize you won't to be teaching him anymore. I'll give him back what he has paid you and I'll make sure they talk off your property, not at your club. But just act normally 'till after the next lesson. Ok?" Steve thanked him.

Saul was the first to stand up. He hugged Steve again and asked him, "You have enough time to go play?" Steve replied that he had time for nine holes but had to leave after that.

Dom stood up. "Why don't you two go play alone. Take some time to catch up." We all agreed and made our way back to the club.

Seeing how Steve and Saul treated each other, it dawned on me that my jealousy towards Rich was because Rich also saw Saul as a second father, not just as a friend. Steve wasn't a threat to my relationship, but Rich was. Steve was Saul's age and I guess that made it different. All I knew, at that time, was that I had to let it go.

At the club, Saul and Steve went out to play and Dom and I spent some time hitting balls on the range. Dom was developing a really good swing and his ball flight, while not exceptionally long, was always the same, very consistent. I was impressed. He always started the first drill with his right foot back on its toe. As Saul said, starting that way gives you balance and tempo and the mindset you need. It's part of getting out of the way of the release.

After about an hour, Dom stepped away to make a call. Although I wasn't purposely eavesdropping, I was close enough that I could hear Dom's side of the call. I knew it was Rich. Dom told him to be here Thursday morning. His voice was different than usual. It was more like someone giving an order that was not to be questioned. It was a tone I'd never heard Dom use before. I was pretty sure it had to do with Steve, but other than that, it was none of my business.

When Steve and Saul finished playing, they joined us on the range. Saul asked Dom to hit some six irons so he could show Steve his progress. Before he started, Saul pulled up a video on his phone. It was of Dom when he first came to Saul. Steve watched it and then watched Dom. He looked at Saul and said, "Wow, that was six months ago? Put together a short game and you'd be tough to beat."

Dom smiled and said, "I'm betting on it." We chuckled and Steve had a realization.

"Oh yeah! The bet with, what's his name, Woody;

Saul told me about that. Dom, you get a short game and you can beat a four handicap. I hope it's more than just one round. Anybody can beat anybody for eighteen if it's their day, but over a longer match the better player always wins. Amateurs usually can't hold together a great run for more than a round."

Steve said his goodbyes again, hugging Saul and thanking Dom for his help. We stayed on the range for another hour and decided to call it a day. I decided to play, and Dom and Saul went to Saul's house saying they had some things to discuss. Before they left, Saul told me to stop by when I was done, and we'd have dinner. I agreed and made my way to the first tee.

Dinner that night was relaxed. Each of us talked about golf and our thoughts on Dom's progress. Saul asked me about how I played today, and I told him I thought pretty well. As a matter of fact, I said, Shot 69 and it could have been a lot better." After dinner, Saul left to go outside, and Dom and I were sitting at the table. I stood up to join Saul on the deck, but Dom asked me to sit for another minute.

"Blu, I need a favor," he said. "I am buying a car from just north of D.C. and I would like you to drive up with Rich. If Rich drives it and approves of it, then he'll drive it back down. If he decides it's not a good buy, then you'll drive with him back here. You can take my car. Will you do that for me?"

"Sure," I told him, "if Saul is good with it." I stepped out to speak to Saul. He told me that I would be leaving at 4 a.m. on Thursday." I said okay and left for the night.

We spent Wednesday morning and the beginning of the afternoon at the course. Then, Dom instructed me to take his car in the morning and pick Rich up in the parking lot at the Villager, same time as what Saul said. The villager is a small sandwich shop in the village of Pinehurst. He took my arm and led me away from Saul. Then, he looked right at me.

"Look and please take this seriously," he said. "You pick up Rich and drive him there. Then, you drive back, either together or in separate cars. Here's the thing, if you stop to eat or get gas, talk to no one. I mean *no one*. You understand?"

"Yes, Dom." I nodded.

"Follow Rich's lead and do what he tells you to, okay?"

"Yes sir."

And Blu, remember the rule about asking questions. Only ask if you really want to know."

"Okay, Dom, no questions, then. I got it."

His parting words to me were, "Play nice with Rich." Dom smiled walked back to the Pro shop where we had left Saul. I turned and walked to the car.

I thought all that night about what it was really about. I didn't think Dom would put me in a bad situation. In the end, I resigned myself to believing that, at worst, it was so Rich could talk with the guy that Steve was concerned about.

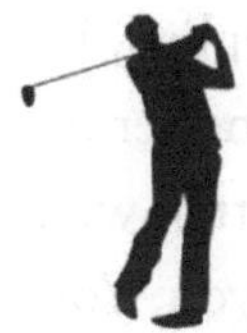

CHAPTER 8

I pulled into the Villager at 4 a.m. Rich was leaning against his car smoking a cigarette. He walked over and jumped in the passenger seat.

He looked at me and smiled. "Road trip for the boys, huh?" He let out a laugh. I smiled back, trying not to encourage him to go on. We got on our way, out of The Village and on towards Route 1 to head north to Virginia. Suddenly, I realized that I knew we were going to Virginia, but I had no idea where in Virginia. I looked over to Rich and he was looking at me, smiling. It was odd. I had no idea why he was smiling.

"You got an address?" I asked.

"I was wondering how long it'd be before you asked," he said. "Yeah, I'll tell you where to go."

About an hour into our trip, Rich looked at me and said, "You don't like me, do you?"

I told him, "I never said that."

"That's not what I asked," he said.

"No, it wasn't," I replied. I kept my eyes on the road.

"Blu, you gonna answer my question?"

"Why does it matter what I think? If you must know, no. I don't like you. You're that guy that's fun to drink with and everybody likes to be around. Always have an answer for everything, but here's one that may stump you: Why don't people trust you? I have no idea what it was between you and Saul, but I am almost positive it had to do with trust. Am I right?"

"You know, Blu. You don't know who Saul was before you met him. He wasn't the person you know now," Rich said. "He's done some things. Hell, we've all done some things that aren't so nice. I'm talking - before his big change. Before he started talking with Steve about God and forgiveness, and all that bullshit." I chuckled at his reference.

"Some people wouldn't think of it as bullshit."

"All this trouble and what does he have to show for it?" Rich responded.

"What like happiness, serenity?" I interjected, almost sarcastically. "You mean like that? You know, some people believe that God can bring them all the joy and peace in life they've ever wanted."

"Not in my world." Rich replied.

"Maybe you need to change worlds," I said. "Look,

Rich, don't start telling me anything about Saul, his past or anything. That goes for Dom, too. I'm not stupid. I know there's more to them than the last six months that I've been around. That doesn't concern me. But, you know, the fact that you feel the need to talk, about their past and things I don't know about, confirms my suspicions that you can't be trusted. I'm sure they wouldn't want you talking about this with anybody." We both turned our heads to the road. "Even me," I added. We didn't talk much after that.

We got on this two-lane country road and Rich told me to turn right into an auto repair shop. There were two guys standing around out front. They were not dressed like mechanics, more like the cast of Godfather. Fat Italians in short sleeve dress shirts and long pants.

"Stay here," Rich said as he got out and greeted the three guys out front. After some talk, one of them pointed to the far side of the building. Rich told him one last thing and pointed down the road. Then, he came back and got in the car.

"Go down to the diner on the left," Rich said, pointing to a building about a quarter mile down from where we were. As he got out, he looked at me and said, "Blu, love me or hate me, you'll be sitting in that diner, ready to go at 12:15 and you wait till I get back."

I said, "Got it."

Instead of doing whatever it was he was going to do, he stood there. "12:15," he said. "Do not fuck this up, understand?"

I nodded again. "Rich, I got it."

At 12:22 I got a call from Rich, telling me to go back to the auto shop. He actually said, "Blu, go now, now! Go right now." I threw a twenty on the table and dipped out to my car. I'd never heard him talk that way before. I could tell he was dead serious.

I sat in my car on the side of the building until I saw him pull up, alone. He was waiting for the garage door to open when I noticed a chip in the paint. I studied it until I realized it was a hole. Hell, it was a bullet hole. As the door opened and he drove in, another car pulled in behind him. It was the guy he was driving with earlier. As he passed, I heard a thumping that disappeared as he drove inside behind Rich. Two minutes later, Rich exited through the side door right in front of me. He had a Grateful Dead tour shirt on and, in one hand, was carrying the shirt he had on earlier and a can of something.

He stopped at a rusty burn barrel that was right in front of my car. He dropped the shirt into the barrel and emptied the liquid contents of the can over the shirt. Then he threw the can in, too, and pulled something out of his pocket. I watched two things, just then, that stuck with me. The first was that he pulled out a match stick and lit it on his jeans like the star in a western movie. Throwing it in the barrel caused flames to erupt from inside. The second was that his arms and hands were stained. He turned and walked over to a spigot outside the building and washed his hands and arms with the hose. He dried his hands on a dirty towel hanging nearby and threw it into the barrel that was still spouting flames.

"Let's go," is all he says. As I pulled away, through the window, I saw one of the guys pointing his arm towards the open trunk of the car that came in behind Rich. Then, two flashes of light, each followed by the popping sound of a gun being fired.

We didn't speak, except for him telling me where to turn. He never told me the route, just the next turn. About two hours into the trip back, he had me pull onto a dirt road that traced the shoreline of a small lake. Halfway around, we stopped. He got out and pulled a gun from behind his belt. My mind was spinning, wondering if he planned on shooting me. He grabbed some wipes from the glove compartment and used one to wipe down the gun in his hand. He turned back to me and smiled. It calmed me a bit and, to this day, I don't know why. He could have been smiling because he likes to kill things and he was imaging the fun it would be to shoot me, the only rival to his and Saul's friendship.

I didn't have those thoughts until later. In one quick movement, he turned and threw the gun into the lake. My heart was racing when he got back in and I said the only thing that came to mind.

"So - not gonna buy the car, huh?"

Rich smiled. "Nah, it had a bullet hole in it." At that, we both broke out laughing. I mean really laughing, like I hadn't done in years, almost to tears. When we'd composed ourselves, I looked back at Rich.

"I'm just glad you didn't shoot me," I admitted.

"Why would I shoot you?" he said. "I need a wheel man."

It occurred to me, just then; that is exactly what I was. A wheelman, fully complicit. And the seduction went on. When we pulled back onto the road, his phone rang. It was Dom.

"Yeah, it's done but not as planned." There was a pause. "He wasn't as agreeable as we assumed, he would be. We had to take another approach. He shot at us; made me decide between him and us, man, I chose us." Another pause. "You're right. Vincent is going to know. It's a whole new problem." He bowed his head a bit. "I'll talk to you tomorrow."

About an hour later, Rich had me pull into an old beaten-up roadside motel that was attached to a restaurant. The place probably thrived some time before the interstate was built, years ago. Rich went inside and came out just a few minutes later. When he got back in, he held out two slips of paper. They were receipts, dated for last night and today.

"Hold on to these," he said. "This is where we were last night and where we ate this morning at eleven. Got it?" I nodded and drove on. We got on the interstate and didn't speak until we pulled into the Villager a couple hours later. Before he got out, he reached into the bottom of his pant leg and took out a gun. "Here, you may want this."

I told him I didn't, so he shoved it into the glove box. "In case you change your mind," he said. He got out and told me to go take the car to Dom and Saul. I pulled up to Saul's house. Dom walked out as I turned off the car. He got in and looked at me.

"Are you ok?" he asked.

I said I was.

"Listen, Blu. Things didn't go as planned with this thing. I'm sure you know that." I nodded as he continued. "Listen, I made a pledge to Saul that you would never be involved in anything that could get you jammed up. I broke that promise with this trip and I'm sorry. Now, you have a decision to make. If you want to walk away, right now, that's okay. If you stay, I'll protect you from this ever happening again, but in this situation, we must be clear. If anyone talks to you, Rich told you what to say. Are you okay with that?"

"Dom," I said. "I am not going anywhere, but is that story as solid as you think? What about cameras, anywhere we stopped? Or the waitress where I had lunch?"

"Blu, there were no cameras anywhere you were. This isn't our first time on the dance floor. As far as the waitress is concerned, don't worry it. The place you dropped Rich; they own the diner. Everyone that works there knows the deal; no one talks. The hotel you got the receipts for; didn't you see the car lot across the street?

That's where Rich went to check out a car for me. That's the whole story."

He reached into his pocket and pulled out a card. "Look, Blu, it's best, if anyone ever wants to talk to you about this, to say nothing. Absolutely nothing. If they're cops, tell them to arrest you or leave you alone. Hand them this card. I know how you think that looks, but trust me, the more you say, the more they will come after you." He paused to watch my face. "Do you understand, Blu?"

"I do, Dom. I'm good," I said. "I am not a child and I'm not stupid. I have a good idea what went down, I got the story and you can count on me. All I ask is one thing. Don't send me anywhere with Rich again. He just fucking scares me. I know it sounds far-fetched, but I thought he was going shoot me."

Dom laughed. "What sounds far-fetched about that?" he said, smiling at me. He saw the look on my face. "I'm just fucking with ya," he laughed. "Well, kind of, but I'll keep him in line. Nothing is gonna happen to you as long I'm around."

"Thanks, Dom," I said.

"The gun, the one Rich gave you, you might want to keep it around. You know, just in case."

"Thanks, but no thanks." We got out and I walked to my car. Before getting in, Dom had one more thing to tell me. "Blu, we're doing breakfast here tomorrow. Come on over when you get up, before 6:30." I nodded and drove home.

I didn't sleep well that night. I wasn't sure about anything now except that everything kept coming to the same conclusion: I wasn't going anywhere. I couldn't. My friends felt more like family and I was happy. I hadn't felt like this since I was a kid. Since before my parents died. I couldn't walk away from any of it.

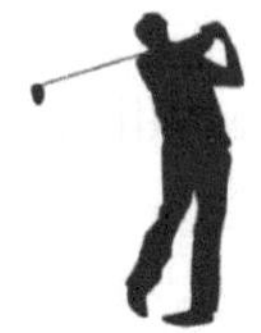

CHAPTER 9

I pulled up to Saul's house the next morning and saw Rich's car in the driveway. My heart sank. I sure as fuck was not looking forward to seeing him. I slammed my car door shut and walked into the house, not knowing what to expect. I didn't see anyone at first, so I went into the kitchen and poured myself some coffee. That's when I heard talking.

Dom and Rich were on the patio and Dom was pissed at Rich. Listening closer, I could hear every word.

"Rich, this is such a fucking problem now. A major fucking problem. You had to fuck it up."

"The guy pulled a gun and shot at us, Dom! What do ya' think I'm gonna do? That fuckin' guy! And for that matter, what the fuck would you have done, huh?"

"Okay, okay, I got it, but…fuck! Vincent knows Hunters is out there somewhere and he's gonna come for him."

"Yeah. And you know who he's gonna have taken care of it?"

"Me, dammit,' Dom put his hand on the back of his head. "He's gonna tell me to do it. It was my responsibility from the start. I was supposed to get rid of him ten years ago. Now, he's gonna put my balls in a vice."

Rich spoke up. "He still blames Saul for his kid being shot."

"He was supposed to be with you, instead of his kid." Dom put his finger on Rich's chest, "But Saul refused; said he can't keep doing it. He wanted to change his life. He told me a story that Steve's wife told him about a dot and a line. He says, 'The dot is your time on earth. The line goes on forever. The line: that's your time with God." He said she asked him what he wants to live for, the dot or the line."

"I really want to shoot Steve for causing Saul to think about all this shit." Rich slapped his leg and let out a litany of expletives.

"No, I see Saul's point," said Dom. "I did what I did so he could get out and have a chance to live his life the way he wanted to."

"What's he turning you too?" Rich asked. Dom paused before answering.

"I'm too far gone…too far for Jesus to want me. I

guess I thought, if I did this for Saul, it would be a way of asking for forgiveness, ya' know? Either way, Saul didn't go, and Vince's kid did, and got shot. Vince still wants Saul dead. I don't know how he got the idea he was alive but, regardless, here we are."

"That's bullshit," said Rich. "Vince's kid's a fucking idiot. He got pissed and just started shooting. No reason to, either. We could have walked away and straightened it out with the 'spics later. But no, he just freaked out. On top of that, he's an awful fucking shot." He took a long drink of whatever was in his glass and dropped it on the table. "So, what. What do we do?"

"We wait to hear from Vince," Dom held his hands into the air. "We wait to figure out what he knows. What the fuck else can we do?" I made my way back to the front door. There was no way I wanted to be a part of that conversation.

That night I left CCNC through the gates, as usual. There was a car parked with two guys in it, right across the street from the guard shack. The same guys I saw in New York when I was caddying for Ben. They watched me as I pulled by. The next morning, I saw their car on the way to Saul's house. They followed me from the Lawn and Tennis Club entrance to the gates of CCNC. They didn't seem to care about being seen, but they turned around, instead of entering the country club. Just to be sure they didn't follow; I drove the long way around the lake before turning onto Saul's street.

When I went in, Saul and Dom were sitting on

the porch and talking over coffee. I said nothing when I stepped outside. I could judge the seriousness of the discussion from the look on their faces.

Eventually, I just went for it. "Guys, I hate to pile it on here, but something's up. I need to talk with you."

Saul asked me to go on and I told them about the guys at the gate last night and again this morning.

Dom put his weight on the table in front of him. "Blu, you need to stay here for a few days until we have a handle on this thing,"

"Leave here tonight," Dom said. "Go home. Pull all your drapes shut so no one can see in. At midnight, go out your back door and through the woods. You know the woods behind your place; go to the street behind your land. Someone will be there to get you and bring you here. Stay here till we work this shit out."

"Should I bring clothes and stuff?" I asked, already thinking of what to pack.

"No, we'll take care of that," Saul said. "Just be there and say nothing."

I nodded. "Okay."

I went home around five o'clock. Two men were walking up towards my front steps. I knew right away they were cops. The taller one spoke first, calling out as he got closer.

"Mr. Jones, can we have a word with you?"

I stood in front of the door. "Depends on what you want."

He pulled out his phone and touched the screen a

few times before turning it to me. "Do you know this guy?"

I saw a picture of a guy I didn't recognize and that's exactly what I told them.

"Do you know a man named Dom Ciacchini?" I knew they knew the answer. "Yes," I said, plainly.

"Mr. Jones, he is a good friend of yours, isn't he?" His tone was getting cockier by the second. "As a matter of fact, you have been seen with him a lot over the last few months."

"Yep," I said. "He's a golfing buddy. I don't know much about him, but we do play a lot of golf."

"Let me tell you a bit about your alleged golfing buddy, Mr. Jones," the other one started in on me. "He is not the man you think he is. He's a real bad guy; a person of interest in no fewer than *seven murders* over the last ten years. What do you have to say to that?"

I looked just at him. From somewhere inside, I felt a rage piling up. He was attacking someone I thought of as family.

"Sir, what do I have to say?"

"I say that's his business. Either he didn't do it, or you suck at your job. Now, please leave me alone."

"Mr. Jones, you can work with us and we can make things easy, or not. We can make your life hard, too. It's your pick."

"Officer, you…"

He cut me off before I could go on. "Detective," he said. I continued. "*Detective*, you see this house and this land, here? I got ten acres. See that pickup?" I pointed. "You know what they all have in common? They're all paid for. My parents died when I was a teenager. Few years after I finished high school school, put a bag on shoulder, and worked my ass off to get everything I got. So, to answer your question, I've had it hard all my life. I don't believe I would know easy if I saw it. I'm going to stick with the devil I know and, before I ask you to leave, do me a favor." I pulled out my wallet and removed the card Dom gave me. "If you want to talk again, call him instead." I handed the rude one the card Dom gave me.

"Kind of an expensive attorney for a guy like you, isn't it?"

"Unless you arrest me, it's your expensive attorney. Now, get off my property and don't come back without a piece of paper saying why you need to be here." The words surprised even me as they exited my mouth. I knew they needed a warrant to dig any deeper, though, and they weren't coming in my home without one. They turned on their heels and got in their car and left.

Later that night, right on time, I walked out of my back door and made my way to the road where Dom said a ride would be waiting for me. When I got there, a four-door sedan was sitting on the side of the road. He flashed his lights when he saw me, so I started towards the car. I walked up to the passenger door and leaned over to look in. The car was dark, and the driver had a ball cap pulled down low.

"Did Dom send you?" I asked.

He nodded, so I got in. That's when I realized it was Rich. I looked at him and he read my face. I wasn't happy to see him, but he smiled anyway.

"Why the long face? After I go to all this trouble to come get your ass?"

"Rich," I responded. "Trouble follows you and I don't want any more trouble."

"Blu, trouble don't follow me. It's scared of me."

He laughed while putting the car in drive to take me back to Dom and Saul's place. I just shook my head. In my mind, I was trying to figure out how I got to this point, with Rich in my life and, more importantly, how to get him back out of it. The more we were around each other the less I liked him. But he was Saul's guy, or Dom's guy that Saul inherited, I'm not sure which. Rich stopped at a stop light and looked at me for a minute, when I finally looked back, he started talking.

"You know Blu, it must be pretty fucking nice to live so blissfully, unaware of the situation you're in."

"What situation is that?" I replied.

"Come on, Blu, I know you're not stupid. I'm pretty sure you decided to ignore it for now, but you can't ignore it forever."

"Why don't you enlighten me on what I seem to be unaware of, then." Rich looked right at me, more serious than before.

"Okay, Blu. Let me start by telling you what you already know." He held up one finger for each point as he made them. "One: Saul, or Hunter, whatever, is supposed to be dead. Two: Dom was supposed to be the one to make that happen. Three: Vince was Dom's boss. He gave the order. And four: Vince knows Saul's alive and he's holding Dom responsible. So, here we are and, if you gave the road ahead any thought, you would be concerned. You should be concerned."

"And why is that?" I shifted in my seat.

"Look at the possibilities going forward. Dom whacks Saul and it's all good, unless Vince whacks Dom for fucking this up the first time. If that happens, your ass is grass, too, because you've been with Dom this whole last year. He don't know what you know if you know anything. He'll kill you just in case. If Dom goes through with hitting' Saul; Saul, a person that has, forever, been closer than his own family. If he does that, he'll kill you for sure. Or, maybe Dom refuses to kill Saul. Then, Vince calls in someone else to hit all three of you and me, too."

"Dom could hit Vince, but he's a made guy, so that could be a problem for Dom. He'd end up getting wacked, anyway. And, again, you'd get hit just for insurance."

"In the end, unless Vince dies of natural causes, we all have a problem. You can hate me all you want, but I may be the only one that can keep your ass alive."

"And why would you do that, Rich?"

"Because it's the only outcome that has me alive at the end." He paused to let that sink it. "Blu, whether you like it or not, there's only one way out of all this. There aint no changing your fucking mind, there aint no running. You, motherfucker, are *all-in*."

I looked at him and thought about what he said. I realized, he was right, but I still didn't like him. I guess, for the time being, he was the devil I knew. We had been sitting at this stop light for like five minutes and not single car came by. He put the car in drive and headed to Saul's. About a minute passed before he thought of something else to say to me.

"Look at the bright side, pal. I could have shot ya' back at the lake." He started laughing again.

When we got back to Saul's house, Dom was there and said he and Rich would be staying at the other house. As they walked past me, Dom stopped and put his hands on the outside of my upper arms, looking me right in the eyes.

"You okay, Blu?"

I nodded, still reeling from Rich's comment.

"Good. Let's have breakfast tomorrow, just us two. I'll pick you up, here, at 6. That alright?"

"Sure, Dom," I replied. "I'll be here."

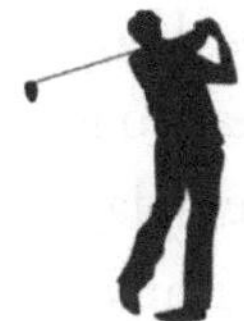

CHAPTER 10

I didn't sleep very well again that night and started my day, early. Dom joined me in the kitchen around 5:30 a.m. He was drinking coffee out of a travel mug. That's when a thought hit me. Here is a guy with all the money in the world. He buys the nicest stuff and his only travel mug costs $1.99 from the Circle K, and you get a free cup of coffee with it. It reminded me of a line in Caddyshack. Rodney says, "What an ugly hat. You buy a hat like this you get a free bowl of soup, heh?" Then looks over at Ted Knights character wearing the same hat and says, "It looks good on you, though!"

Dom stood up and asked if I was ready to go. We made our way to the car and were off. It was not quite light out yet and you could feel rain in the air when the breeze hit you. We turned onto Morganton Road, then U.S. 1 North, then left onto Pennsylvania Avenue. He said he wanted gas and directed me to pull into the store on the left. I wasn't really paying attention too much to where we were going. I concentrated on the car that was following us. Same two guys in the same car that I had been seeing for a few days.

I pulled up to the pump and Dom said he was going inside to pay and for me to pump the gas. A moment later, the pump turned on and I saw the outline of the car in the pre-dawn moonlight. The headlights were out but the inside dash was illuminated. Dom was inside, talking to the cashier. He was standing still looking right at the attendant, but he wasn't responding or moving like he would if he was listening to him. That's when I realized he was looking over the guys shoulder out the window at the car that was following us.

Just then I looked back across the street and saw two dark forms move out of the shadows on either side of the car. They approached the car and raised their arms. Flashes erupted from their hands, but the only sound was glass breaking and dropping onto the asphalt. I stood there, stunned, trying to figure out what it was. It was like a gun shot but muffled. Oh, man. They were using silencers.

I stood there and tried to come to terms with what I had just witnessed. It was murder. It wasn't even *just* a murder; it was a fucking hit. Dom opened the driver's door and said sternly, "Blu, let's go." I noticed that the figure by the driver side door had opened the door, pushed the now-dead driver to the middle, and got in. The other guy ran back down the side street and the car's lights turned on as I buckled myself in. Dom pulled out and, before he turned onto the street, the car with broken windows drove right by us. The driver looked over and gave us a nod. It was Rich. Then another car pulled out of the side street and followed Rich. As he passed, he nodded also. I was astonished to see Kenny driving. Dom pulled out and went back down US-1 towards Southern Pines. He pulled into the parking lot of an all-night breakfast place.

We sat down and the reality of what Rich had said to me last night came creeping in. He was right. I was in this mess and there were no other options. We sat inside and ordered our food while Dom stared at the mostly empty parking lot.

"Blu," he said. "There's something you need to know. When Saul met you and asked you to work for him, he had no intention of this happening. He worries about you and how you are handling the situation. I don't mean that he's worried you will you rat someone out or talk, I mean he wants to be sure you're okay. He loves you like family; like a son." He paused and looked at me. "You need to know that."

I nodded. "Thank you, Dom," I mumbled. "I'm glad you told me." He looked back out the window, but I kept my eyes on him. "Can I ask something?"

"Blu, all pretense is pretty much gone by now, isn't it?" he said. "Ask away."

"Those guys following us, do they have something to do with this Vincent guy?"

Dom looked up from his coffee, not saying anything, so I went on.

"I overheard you and Rich talking at the house when you didn't know I was there."

Dom smiled and reached over to grab my ear with his thumb and a forefinger. He rubbed it a few times then let go. Then he smiled and said, "Strange."

I ask what.

"I was checking to see if you're still wet back there." He paused. "Blu, do you really think that I had a conversation about a crime with Rich and you just happened to overhear it, by chance?"

I laughed. "I'm catching up, slowly," I said. Then I asked, "So, what happens to those guys and their car?"

"They go to the beach today on a wrecker then on a barge out to sea tomorrow night."

"And me?" I asked.

"Well, Rich kind of spelled it out for ya'. I'm sure," Dom said. "There is no out now. There's no running or hiding because I can't trust that. You can't trust what someone might do if they're scared. So, here is the question you need to answer." He shoved a forkful of food into his mouth. "I know you have no blood relatives. We are probably the closest thing to family you have. Someone asked me this question thirty years ago: Would you rather live one day with family or a lifetime with strangers?" He took a drink of coffee and put the cup down again. "Once you know that answer, you'll know what to do."

We finished eating in silence. When we got to the car, I stopped and went over to Dom and, without a word, I put my arms around him and hugged him. I don't know what he thought about it, but I meant it. I stepped away and nodded at him. He nodded, too and we got into the car. Nothing more needed to be said.

The next few days were all pretty much alike. Saul and I went to the club and for breakfast around eight in the morning and then worked on our short game for a couple hours. After a half-hour break and we'd go to the range and, each day, Saul would have a game for us play against each other. His favorite was to would pick targets to hit to, but you could only use a five iron. Here's the real catch: the targets had to be inside of a hundred and fifty yards. Much shorter than either of us hit a 5 iron. Also, we had to take a full swing and the ball had to draw, meaning curve right to left.

"Blu, if you can hit a 5 iron a hundred and twenty yards with a full swing *and* draw the ball close to the hole... Well, you, sir, can golf your ball." The only phrases he ever used to describe a good golfer were 'he's a player' or 'he can golf his ball'. I liked those terms. They just had a feel to them; very satisfying.

Dom would show up each day just after lunch and join us. He was a different Dom, now, always had this hard look on his face. It was the look of a man that had a lot on his mind. I knew he did, so I just respected it and went about my day. On Thursday, Dom showed up for breakfast like he used to. He was happy; he smiled a lot. It was nice to see. It felt like things might finally get back to normal, like it was before the cops.

Sometime around one in the afternoon, I was alone with Saul and mentioned how nice it was to see Dom in a better mood.

He looked at me and smiled. "Maybe."

I was watching Dom and I didn't understand his remark, so I asked Saul what he meant. He grabbed my arm and lead me to a table nearby. There were two wooden chairs at the table and Saul motioned for me to sit. Once we were both sitting, he just stared at me for a moment. He inhaled and then huffed out a loud exhale.

"It's important you know, Blu, I never intended for you to be in the situation we're in right now. You are my best friend and, if I'm honest, the only true friend I have." I started to speak, but he raised his hand with a finger in the air to stop me. "I'll explain in a minute," he said. The pause went on for so long, I finally just asked, "Why is Dom being happy not good?"

"Blu, I am not sure how much you know, but I think you are pretty much up to speed. You spoke with Rich, right."

I nodded.

"Well, I know Rich and I am certain he didn't sugar coat anything. That man can be irritating as fuck, but he has a way of cutting through the bullshit. That can be helpful at times, even when you don't want to hear it. He's not much for letting anyone waste time on things that just aren't real." He looked at me and I guess I smiled a little.

"Yeah, he can be a dick." Saul laughed.

"When is he *not* a dick?" I asked.

"Blu, he isn't really," said Saul. "As a matter of fact, he may be one of the most honest people I know. He will tell you how it is, without ever considering whether or not you want to know." I kept my mouth shut. There must be more to Rich then I've seen.

"Now, back to Dom. Dom has been my friend for over thirty years. I love the guy and I am sure he feels the same. But Dom is not altruistic by nature. I mean that he, sure as hell, is not going to fall on his sword for me. Him being happy means he has decided on a plan to go forward. That plan may be good for me and you and it may not. The only thing I am sure of is that it's good for Dom. Or, at least he thinks it is." Saul fiddled with the ash tray on the table.

"Don't take that the wrong way," he continued. "A lot of people over the years will tell you, "I would die for you," or some other bullshit. Let me tell you right now, those motherfuckers are lying. If you find one person in your life that would do that, you are one lucky S.O.B."

"Wait, if that's true, aren't you worried?"

"Blu, I haven't been worried for coming up on ten

years now." I tilted my head trying to figure out the timeline from what I'd heard so far.

"Let me tell you a story." Saul put his hands together and leaned towards me. "About, I don't know, maybe twelve years ago, Steve called and asked me to go with him to a course called Rock Barn, over in Statesville. He had a qualifier for a tour event there, so I went. I ended up carrying his bag. He said he wanted me there to keep him from overthinking.

"Anyway, he missed the cut by a shot and wanted me to go to Asheville with him. He said he had to meet someone and wanted to play a new course up there while we were there." Saul rolled his shoulders before continuing.

"So, I agreed to go and off we went. I was tired from the round even though it was only about two in the afternoon and Asheville was only an hour and a half away. So, Steve was driving, and I was just looking at the mountains as we got further into them, nodding in and out of sleep. Finally, I woke up as we were turning into a gated area. I looked over too late to see the name of the complex. We drove in front of a building and parked. As I got out, I saw a chapel on the left side of the building we parked in front of. We walked to the entrance of the building and I got this sense that something was off. Not that we were in danger, just… *off.* I can't explain it any better than that. So, we walked into this building, this office building. As we approach the receptionist, Steve speaks up and asks her if 'he' is in. The woman tells him, "Yes sir, he's been waiting for you." So, we walk into this large office and off to the side there is an oval coffee table with four chairs around it. Sitting in one of the chairs is none other than Billy Graham. He stands up, hugs Steve and then, turning to me, he introduces himself. He said my name like he knew me. That didn't seem strange at the time, which was strange in itself."

"So, he starts speaking as if he thought I called him to talk to me about my life. I'll never forget his voice. I never was able to come up with a word that really describes it. It's like thunder and honey; that voice shook you up, then sucked you in and made you feel safe about everything. I remember, at one point, I felt like crying. I wasn't just happy; I mean, I almost lost it. It was the kind of happiness only children feel. More like…joy." Saul went quiet for a moment. "Yeah, pure joy."

"After about an hour of talking, he pulled a piece of paper out of his shirt pocket, put it on the table and wrote something on it. Then, he folds it up and hands it to me. When I reached out to take it from him, he grabbed my hand and looked me straight in my eyes." I could tell Saul was enjoying the reminiscing. He continued, "After a bit of a pause, Mr. Graham says, "Hunter, I need to you to promise me something. I want you to read this note aloud, once, every day and every night. I am not asking you to mean what it says when you repeat it, just read it. Read it out to yourself. On the top, I wrote a date on it. Next to that, I want you to write the date of when you've said this and meant it for the first time."

"I asked what will happen if I never mean it. He smiled and looked at Steve. They both chuckled and Mr. Graham says, 'There's not much chance of that happening.' They both started laughing like it was some inside joke, which, it was. Honestly, that kind of pissed me off then, but how pissed off can you be around Billy Graham, right?"

When Saul finished, he slid the folded piece of paper across the table to me. I unfolded it and looked at it.

07/13/07   12-25-09

Dear God,

I know I'm a sinner, and I ask for your help.
I believe Jesus Christ is Your Son.
I believe that He died for my sin and
that you raised Him to life.
I want to trust Him as my Savior and follow
Him as Lord, from this day forward.
Guide my life and help me to do your will.
I pray this in the name of Jesus.
Amen

Saul pointed to the date on the top and said, "That's the day I gave up trying to figure this out alone. I was so tired of my life and everything. Steve convinced me that it didn't have be that way."

"What got you to that point?" I asked, almost afraid to find out.

"About 11:30pm on Christmas Eve, Rich and I had to meet some people. They showed up at the warehouse some forty-five mins late. They didn't have the money they were supposed to have and one of the guys started trying to talk his way out of it. We weren't having any of it and, out of nowhere, the other guy started shooting, hit me two times in my side." Saul pointed with his thumb to just under his armpit.

"Before I knew what was happening, Rich pulls out two pistols from behind his back and shoots them both right in the center of their foreheads. Then he walked over to me and asked if I could walk. I thought I could. He went over the guy who was talking, took off his coat and hat, and put them on. He got me on my feet and out to the parking lot and to the car that the guys from inside drove. He helped me into the passenger seat. So, he's driving, and he makes a call to get someone to clean up the warehouse and all I could think was: 'Damn, I don't want die in this 'spic's pimped-out Buick.'"

"Rich pulled up to the emergency entrance of the hospital and got out with his hat pulled down low, hiding his face. He called 911 and told someone that I was outside and have been shot in a full Hispanic accent 'n everything. Next thing, the hospital staff is all over the car, putting me on a stretcher. They wheeled me in and, right as I went through the doors, I caught a glimpse of Rich walking into the trees by the road, taking off the jacket and jumping into a car that had just pulled up." Saul leaned back from the table to take a deep breath.

"Well, Blu, there you have it. I know Billy's note by heart by now and not once did I truly mean it till right before I passed out that day. I remember saying it." His eyes got kind of glassy. "I said it and I meant every word of it."

"I woke up a few days later and I remember feeling like I didn't have a care in the world. That week, Dom came to see me, and I told him I wanted out. He tried to tell me all the reasons I couldn't leave, but I didn't care. More than that, I wasn't worried, at all. All the bullshit I was wrapped up in, I just didn't care anymore, ya' know? That was the first time I felt at ease in years and I haven't looked back since." He leaned back towards me and put his finger on the table.

"Every day I say that prayer and I mean it every single time." He handed it to me and saying, "Take it, Blu. I know it will help."

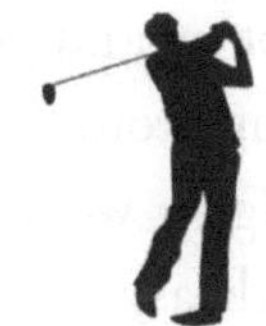

CHAPTER 11

It's strange how quickly I've adjusted to this new life. I knew there was no part of me that considered leaving. Looking back, I realized that I believed I would die in this new life. Now, what really gets me, what stands out the most, is that I was at completely at peace with that.

Life went on. Every day, we ate breakfast together then went to the range or the putting green. Saul would make a practice schedule the night before and give it to us at breakfast. It was made up of four forty-five-minute sessions and we would always have two or three of them on the putting green. Wedges or putts was what he kept drilling into us. I say 'us' because although I was there to watch Dom at first to help him, it had changed to

Saul teaching both of us. I can't really figure when it changed, but it did.

Those were some of the best days of my life. It felt like hanging out with friends from grade school. I was never worried. I just got up and played all day with two guys I really loved being around.

Every Saturday night, we'd go to a pool hall in Sanford called the Speakeasy. It was good pool with real good players, but what we really liked about it was the back room. You wouldn't know it was there unless you knew how to get in. The wall opened up like a secret passageway. The door was invisible and in the hallway by the restrooms. There was a catch, though: once you went in, you weren't coming out until everyone was ready to leave.

This was where the big money games were played. The room was big and had pool chairs around both tables. They were like bar stools only on one side it had a cut out to lean your stick into and it had a wide flat arm rests with cup holders. Saul and Dom loved that room. As did Rich whenever he came with us or met us there. They loved pool and betting and even more, the unique feature that brought them to the pool hall to begin with.

The Days Inn was next door and owned by the pool hall guy's brother-in-law. As if the existence of the room wasn't enough, in keeping with the trend of the 1920's, there was a functioning tunnel from that hidden room to a basement level room in the hotel. After Charlotte,

Saul and the others couldn't take any chances and a set up like that meant they didn't have to.

One of those Saturday nights, after about a month of things being quiet, we went there, to the Speakeasy. Sanford was about a forty-five minute drive. We were there for about an hour. I didn't go in the back this time because I was more interested in talking up one of the waitresses. She was pretty in that girl-next-door sort of way and this was the closest I'd came to a date in a while. We were getting along just fine when some guy walked in. He was tall and slender with his white hair combed straight back. He caught my attention when he walked past my table and stood at the bar, right in front of me.

He took out his phone. "Dom, it's Vince. I'm at the bar, where the fuck are you?" He Italian accent was coming on, thick. "Hurry the fuck up. I aint got all night."

This was the Vince I had heard about. I watched him, ignoring the girl, and he never once noticed me. You would think he'd know who Dom was spending his time with, I thought to myself. I figured a guy like him had to have guys feeding him info. That is, unless he depended on Dom to do all that.

Dom came in the front door five minutes later and walked right up to Vince at the bar. Nobody was around them. I was barely close enough to hear as Dom and Vince shook hands. Vince did not mince any words.

"You gonna clean up this fucking mess you made with our guy, Dom?"

"Listen, Vince, I don't work for you anymore." Dom was pissed. "I'll take care of it because it was my responsibility, not because of your son. Let's just get things out on the table once and for all so you can let this shit go. It was you that sent your son with Rich and, with all due respect, he was a dumb motherfucker, and he got shot because of it." Vince got agitated, but Dom kept talking.

"If you want me to do this, it will be the day after my match with Woody. Kenny s the hitter and Rich will be around just in case something goes wrong. And you; you need to be somewhere with a lot of people when it goes down."

Vince got a dark look in his eye. "No. Fuck that. I'm gonna watch that bastard die," he said, adamantly.

"Fine. But, Kenny's gonna meet with you and tell you how it's gonna go down. Stay with him and *stay out of the way*. If you fuck this up, I'll kill you myself. I am not doing time cause of you. You got it?" Dom's eyes grabbed ahold of Vince and held him for a few seconds. "You got that, Vince?"

"I got it." They shook hands and Vince went to pull away, but Dom tightened his grip.

"After this, we are done." Vince nodded, but Dom hold on for another second. "*Done.*"

Vince nodded again and Dom released his grip. Vince turned and walked out.

I was putting things together. I realized that Dom, at one time had worked for Vince; that he was there to do things that Vince didn't want to touch. He did all the ruthless things that their business needed, the same things that Rich did for Dom. What struck me the hardest in this realization was that Vince, at that moment, saw that he had instilled a beast in Dom; a beast that even himself had lost control over. As Dom turned from the bar, he looked right at me. He slowed his movement, just for a second, to catch my eye and winked before continuing out the door.

Dom had wanted me to hear everything. I was not sure why. Either he wanted me to know when this thing was happening, or he wanted to emphasize that there was no running from this web. Looking back, it was probably both.

The next few days went by quickly. We played and practiced golf, every day. My mind would constantly replay the where and when of how everything was supposed to go down. I would forget about it for short periods of time, only to have it all come rushing back to me. It was the worst at night. I was constantly thinking about it. I didn't sleep more than two hours at a time. I would get caught up thinking about my life and how I'd managed to find myself in the situation I was in.

I thought back to the question Dom gave me: Would you rather live one day with people that love you, or a year with strangers?

Here I am, in my forties, single, and, until Saul, all

the people I had in my life were strangers. I've dated nice girls here and there and always broken it off, never any emotional breakups though. It was just that being with them only distracted me from the emptiness. I wasn't *really* with them. My whole view of the world was changing, and, at that moment, I didn't mind. All I cared about was losing my new life. Rich was right, I was all in.

One night, I cried so hard it exhausted me. I don't remember the last time I cried in bed. This night, though, my tears were tears of joy. Since my parents passed, I hadn't allowed myself to love or to even form bonds. I never wanted to feel the pain of loss, or the absence of those bonds, again. So, I just stopped myself from getting close to anyone. I understood, for the first time, that my life was what I made of it. I thought I was saving myself pain, but really, I was slowly killing myself. These people entered my life and, for the first time in twenty years, I allowed another person to touch my soul. I was certain that losing them was very possible, but I wasn't going to let that get in my way.

I was all in.

One night, weeks later, I pulled up to my house to the same investigators from before, waiting at my front door. I was certain they were going to arrest me for something but had no idea for what. I told them the last time to either bring a warrant or to stay off my property. Now, they were back. Shit.

I got out of the car. "May I help you?" I said.

The tall one told me they wanted to talk with me, and asked if they could come in.

"Well," I said. "Since you're already trespassing, you might as well."

"Look," he said. "We are just trying to help you. Sorry if you don't see it that way."

I went to the kitchen table and sat down. One of them did the same and the other stood, looking at the room. The one sitting pulled out a picture from a file and set it in front of me, asking, "You ever seen this man before?"

"Not that know of."

"What kind of answer is that?" he said.

"Look," I said. "I was at Walmart on Saturday and probably saw two hundred people or more. I think I would recognize probably ten of them at the most, but I don't know any of them. So, if you want to know if I know this person the answer is no. If you want to know if I have seen this person, the answer is not that I know of."

He then turned over another picture. It looked like it was the same guy, but he was dead and some of his face was eaten away.

"This guy was found buried in his car with his friend here." The detective turned over another, similar picture but of a different guy. "Their bodies were dug up by red wolves. These same two guys were seen leaving behind you from CCNC. Can you explain that?" They must have meant while they were following me.

"I don't have any idea. Hold on," I sat down in my chair, "Let me make a call. I might be able to help you."

I picked up my phone and called the attorney's number that Dom gave me. Mike Brown was his name and all I knew was that he started as an injury/DUI-type attorney and had a real hatred for cops.

He started representing guys like Dominic and his type; mob guys. He was good and he had no respect for the system. He would show up for court in jeans and, as I heard it, got a judge's reprimand and was held in contempt for not agreeing to dress differently for a trial. He would sue anybody for, seemingly, outrageous reasons and win. His receptionist answered my call. "Is Mike in? This is Blaise Jones."

"Yes, just one moment, Mr. Jones." Piano music played in her absence. A minute in, Mike picked up.

"Hello, Blu, how can I help you?"

"I'm here with two police investigators that are asking about two guys they found dead that, I guess, were following me."

Mike cleared his throat. "Blu, are these the same investigators that were at your place before?"

"Yes sir." I glanced at the officers. They were listening intently to my side of the conversation.

"Blu, hold on one second; don't say a word. I'm going to conference someone in."

I heard the beeps of him entering the number. While he dialed, I looked at the officers, nodded and smiled. A baritone male voice answered.

"This is Commander Glen speaking. How can I help you, Mr. Brown?"

"Well, we have a problem. Two of your finest are sitting with my client, Mr. Blaise Jones, who is on the line with us, now. He told these two not to come back on his property or bother him without a warrant. Low and behold, they're right back, trespassing on his property, harassing a law-abiding citizen of this great state. And, all of which, you can be sure got recorded on video." I heard a sigh from the Commander's end of the conversation.

"Their names please, Mr. Brown?"

"Mr. Jones, are these the same men as last time?" Mike asked me.

I told him, "Yes sir."

He continued, "I believe the one in charge is called Adams, Commander."

"I will handle it, Mr. Brown," said Commander Glen. "Mr. Jones, I apologize for any inconvenience."

I heard the click of his phone exiting the call.

Mike spoke again. "Blu, put your phone on speaker." I did as he said.

"Hello boys, I am Mr. Brown, Mr. Jones' attorney. You should remember my name as he gave you my card the last time you visited. I want to be sure that I have everything clear. Who is the arresting officer, today?"

Adams straightened up in his chair. "We are not arresting Mr. Jones, today. We only asked to visit with him concerning a murder that he's been tied to."

"You misunderstand," Mike Brown said, "I was asking who is going to be placing the two of *you* under arrest for trespassing and harassment of my client. You have been here before; you were asked to leave and not comeback without a warrant. Further, my client gave you my card as his attorney and I was to be contacted if you wished to speak with him again." Adams tried to interrupt but Mike went on. "I will give you the benefit of my assessment of this situation and give you some good advice." He paused.

Just then I heard a cell phone ring. Before the officer could react, Mike said, "I'd advise you to answer that call.' Adams looked at his phone and his face went white. He answered it and started in on a string of 'yes-sirs' to the Commander on the other end of the call. Adams nodded to his partner and they both stood up, exited the kitchen, and continued out the door, without stopping. When the door shut, I mumbled, "Wow," under my breath.

"Are we good?" Mike asked.

"Yes sir," I said.

Mike chuckled and told me to call him if I ever saw those two again. Then, he hung up. I sat there in shock for a moment or two before busting out laughing. Talk about brass balls; this guy must sound like a cow when he walks. I told Dom and Saul about it the next day, but they already knew and that didn't surprise me. This was my life, for better or worse.

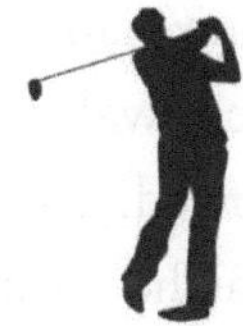

CHAPTER 12

The following Sunday, we went back to the Old North State Club in Baden, North Carolina. The same place we went to after the pool hall in Charlotte. I knew we were here because it was secluded and because, other than Rich, nobody knew we were here. I thought: what if someone followed Rich? Nobody's that stupid, though. If he saw someone behind him for a few miles he would lead them off course and see if they were following him. If they were, he'd turn the car around and ram them head on. He had a reputation for crazy shit like that. Saul told me once, he said, "Sometimes, Rich will do something so fucking crazy just to show everyone he could. That was enough to make sure nobody fucked with him."

Things had calmed down a bit, but Dom's mood seemed to be a lot more serious. During the day, he was deeply focused on his game. Rich showed up daily to talk with him. What was different now was that they were always talking alone; Saul was never involved. He would see the two of them walking off to talk alone, but he never seemed concerned. I wasn't sure why. Maybe Dom had told him that he would handle it and Saul trusted him to protect us. Or maybe, he really was that deeply invested in his belief in God that he just accepted any outcome as God's will. I don't know, but I do know he didn't look worried.

I wanted to ask him, or warn him, or do something. I didn't know what. It was so confusing. That's when it occurred to me that, maybe, he knew there was no escape from what was coming, and he just wanted to enjoy his last days on a golf course with the people he loved. Dom's words came back to me. "I'd rather live a day with people I love than a lifetime with strangers."

It went on like this until Friday, the day before the match. We were going to CCNC that evening. After breakfast at the house, we went to the course. Dom and I were on the range and Saul was practicing his short game. Rich drove up in a golf cart with Kenny next to him. I didn't notice anything off until they walked over. I glanced over where Saul was. He had stopped and was watching intently. I could see the outline of guns on the back of Rich and Kenny's pants, under their shirts. I knew they always carried, but neither one was even trying to hide it. I kept my focus on them and Saul. I was trying to figure out what was so different; what made Saul take notice. Then I realized, it was Kenny. Kenny being there meant either there was a problem, or something was going down, and soon.

Then, I remembered Rich told me Kenny's nick name was 'The Plumber.' You only call him when shit's going down. Rich told me that a few months ago. I thought it was a funny phrase back then. I'm not laughing now.

The three talked for about half an hour and Saul never once hit a shot. He just watched. They broke up and Rich and Kenny left. Dom walked over to Saul and spoke for a minute then said he had to go. He told us we were to drive back at 6pm and that he would be at the house an hour before.

Now, I was nervous. In my mind, as long as Dom was with us, we were safe. I felt sure that he wouldn't let anything happen to me or Saul. I walked to the clubhouse, watching Saul, who was hyper-vigilant, almost Argus-eyed with his head on a swivel. He was paying attention to everything around him. When I walked into the grill room, I took a seat by a window that had a perfect view of everything happening outside.

After about ten minutes of watching, someone tapped me on my shoulder. I jumped a bit. When I turned, I saw it was the Assistant Pro. He was looking at me, a little shocked himself.

"I'm sorry to disturb you, Mr. Jones, but I have a message for you."

I just stared at him. He had this blank, unemotional look on his face, like a character in a Stephen King movie. He lifted his hand with a note in his palm.

"You have a private call." He repeated. I still didn't get what he was saying as I took the note from him. It had a phone number with a 301-area code. I asked him who it was from. He said, again with the same blank look on his face, "Someone who wants to speak to you, privately." I nodded and he walked away.

I looked around to see if anyone was watching but no one was around. I walked down a side hallway and pulled out my phone.

I called the number and a man answered after the first ring. I recognized the voice, but I wasn't sure from where. "Hello," I responded, "this is Blaise Jones. I was given a message."

"Blu, this is Steve, Saul's friend. Blu, listen, a guy came here on Friday. He was a friend of the person I was teaching, the one that made me call Dom and come down a few months ago, if you remember. He told me he was coming back on Sunday. He said he knows Hunter's alive and he's sure I know where he is. I wanted to call Dom, but if this guy found out, I don't know what would happen."

"Steve, is your family safe?"

"Yes, I sent them away," he said. "They will be fine, for now."

"I'll talk with Dom. I'll call you after. Is that okay?"

"Yeah."

"Steve, till then, if anyone shows up, just do what they say."

"Okay."

I hung up and went to find Dom. He was sitting on a bench at the driving range, alone. Saul was still at the practice green, hitting wedges. I asked Dom if we could talk. He motioned with his hand for me to sit and I did. He had a calm look on his face. I had never seen this look on him before. He was a confident guy. You know, when he was in a room, he *was* the room. Everyone could feel his presence. But now, he was more like a man fishing alone on a pier. It felt, and I might be reading too far into it, like he was unhappy with the situation and resigned to it, all the same. I don't know if I was right, even today, but I do know that he was not happy.

"What can I do for you, my friend?" he asked without turning his head or revealing any emotion. That made me uneasy. I knew he looked at us as friends, but that phrase didn't fit the Dom I knew. My heart started beating faster. I didn't know any of the situation's pieces or players and that scared me. I told him about my phone call with Steve and all he said was, "I see." He didn't say anything else for a while, then he turned and looked at me. He reached out and took my hand.

"Call him back and tell him to say nothing. *Nothing.*

Tell him, if a man comes, to go with him. Don't fight and don't run."

"How do you know he will take Steve or where he'll take him?"

"Because. That's what I would do." Then he paused for a second and, still looking at me, said, "That goes for you, too. You do what you're told, Blu. Don't fight and don't run." Chills ran down my back.

After another moment, Dom looked back down the range and asked, "Do you ever think Steve and Saul know what they're talking about? I mean look at him over there. Saul is so calm. He knows what's coming and still he seems to be at peace. I've known him for years, but this last year; he's different. Every damn day, he's happy. I haven't had twenty-four hours in a row without worry since I was ten."

"And so, it goes." He turned to me with his old familiar expression back. "Blu go now. Go and do what I told you."

I went out to the end of the practice tee so that no one could hear me. I called Steve and told him what Dom had told me to say. He agreed. Then, right as I was going wish him good luck, he cut me off with something that still sticks with me, today.

"Blu, I'm not stupid," he said. "I have a family so I can't go anywhere, but you can, Blu. You can run and keep running. I have known these guys for a while and this isn't going to end well. I wish you the best, Blu. I mean it. God bless you."

I hung up and walked back to where Dom was hitting balls. He stopped when I got to him. He gave me a look, waiting for me to tell him about the call.

"I told him what you said," I explained. "I guess he's scared for his family."

"There's a lot of that going around," Dom said softly, turning back to address another shot.

Around 4:30 that evening, I was getting my clubs together and into the car. Saul was with me, but I had not seen Dom for hours. We packed up the car and drove back to the house. When we got there, I saw Rich's car parked. Rich, Kenny, and Dom were in the driveway, talking. We walked up and greeted them. Kenny asked how I was doing. "I'm alright," I told him. He stepped closer and hugged me so he could whisper. "I will try to protect you," Kenny warned, "but if you do some crazy shit, I can't help you. Do what you're told so I can know where you stand and what to expect."

He ended the hug and pulled a gun from his pocket. Looking at me, he said, "It's the one from your car that Rich gave you. Don't ever be caught without it until I take it back." I nodded and tried to take it, but he held his grip. "*Never* without it. Understand? If you take a shit, it's on you. Got it?" I nodded again. He pulled away and smiled. "Well, alrighty then!" he said, turning to everyone else, "let's do this thing."

He opened Rich's car door and got in. We all followed his lead. I went with Dom and Saul while Rich and Kenny drove separately.

The drive down was quiet. Saul, looking out the window, commented on the sod farm we passed on 211. The man that owned it was Al Williams, my godfather. Al looked like a regular blue-collar guy, living paycheck to paycheck, but he was worth millions. I thought about Clay.

Saul started saying something about building a course that was perfectly flat like the farm. No trees, and the only hazards were the pot bunkers placed strategically on the course. He said the pot bunkers would be placed so that once you're in, you can only pitch it ten yards or so.

The greens would be mounded making them drain into the green side pot bunkers. The same bunkers would be from tee to green with wicker baskets instead of flags at the hole so the wind couldn't be gauged. Then, he paused and said, "No yardage books, just a hundred-fifty marker in the middle of the fairway." Dom broke out laughing.

"Fuck, Saul!" he exclaimed. "Why don't you just shoot him in leg on the first tee and wish him good luck? Nobody's gonna play that course more than once."

"I know," Saul said. "Wouldn't it be wonderful?"

Dom kept laughing and I joined in. I saw what Saul envisioned. Just a quiet golf; no one around to screw it up. I leaned forward from the back. He was right, it would be wonderful.

"Could call it *Heaven*," I said to him.

"Yeah. That's perfect," he mumbled, still dreaming of his course.

I leaned back, also caught up in Saul daydream. I realized Saul's heaven would be perfect for me, too.

We had just settled in at the CCNC house when I got a call. It was Mike Kell. He was the guy from Peak'n Peek in New York when I caddied for Ben on the Web.com tour. He said he was in town for the match and asked if I could meet for a beer at the Pine Crest Inn, an old, quaint hotel in the Pinehurst Village. I said yes and we decided to meet that night at eight.

I told Dom where I was going, and he suggested I take Rich with me. I paused for a second, wondering how I could get out of taking him. The expression on Dom's face told me it wasn't a request.

What Steve told me was still on my mind. I was trying to string together the what ifs. What if I did run. Where would I go? How would I pay for anything without leaving a trail? I needed to use cash because the cops, the crooked ones, and the good ones, could track any credit card to me. If I needed cash, I knew my house and land was worth half a million. That meant I just needed five or ten-grand to hold me over till closing. I had way more than that in my safe at home. It was all the cash Saul had given me over the last year.

Then, there were other things to consider. I had to stay off the grid: no credit cards or bank accounts; numerous cell phones, all burners. It wouldn't go on forever; it couldn't. Eventually, I would need a new identity, one with no ties to me. Then, it hit me.

Clay.

It was a long shot, but I had his wallet and his Social Security card, his license and birth certificate.

Ever since all that went down with Clay and Doug, I wasn't the same. I thought of it often and was scared it would come back to bite me in the ass. But now, I was thinking that it might have happened for another reason. Like, it might just save my ass. If I decided to run; if I got somewhere far away where no one knew me; if the DMV in that small town had limited resources; and if I befriended the person at the DMV, would they overlook any technical issues? Maybe.

I thought about how much he looked like me. With this picture on his license, no one would question it twenty years later. Would they?

I had enough cash from Saul to run and the first half of a plan, but I still wasn't sure. I didn't know if I would get the chance to be alone before Monday. If I did get the chance, could I run. Was I even ready? I told myself I would make that decision when, and if, the moment came. That might be the stupidest way to plan your future, but I wasn't ready to give all this up. Not yet.

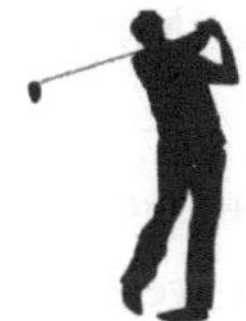

CHAPTER 13

ike was sitting at the bar when I walked in and raised his glass to me. I walked over and sat down on the stool to his left. Rich was already seated on the other side of the bar. Mike smiled at me. When I was settled, he asked, "How are you, pally?"

Pally. I had heard him use the term before and seemed to be a term of endearment. Not one I had heard before, but whatever.

"Just fine, Mike," I replied. "And to what do I owe the pleasure of your company, this fine Carolina evening?"

"Oh, you know why I'm here," he said. "Don't think for a second I was going to miss this match. I've known both those guys for years. Dom couldn't play a lick a year ago, but if I know him as I'm sure I do, he can damn well play now. My only question to you, my friend, is who has he been working with?"

"I can't tell you that Mike. I'm sorry, but that's his business."

He smiled and grabbed my arm, leading me to a table in the corner. As we sat, he never took his eyes off me. With no one in earshot, he leaned forward and whispered, "It's true, isn't it, Blu? He's alive, isn't he?"

"Who are talking about, Mike?" I asked. "Who's alive?"

Hunter," he said. "He was my friend. I loved him, man, and I never believed he was dead. Not for one second."

"I don't know anyone by that name," I said. "I am truly sorry you lost your friend. If I could help you out, I would, but I can't."

He looked at me while raising his beer to his mouth. I could see him measuring my words, not just understanding what I said, but what I didn't say.

"I guess I could be mistaken," he responded. "What do you think, Blu. Do you think I'm wrong?"

"Well, I don't know you that well, but you don't strike me as a person that makes assumptions without doing your research. You also don't seem like you're wrong all too often."

"I hope you're right; I really do. Blu, if you're right about me and I'm right about this, well, that would make me very happy." His smile grew as he sat back in his chair and took another drink.

"Mike, again, I don't know who you are talking about, but he must have made an impression on you. I hope you are right; that he is alive, I mean."

"Oh, he made an impression, alright. When I first met Hunter, we played a match and he beat me, seven and six or something. After, when we shook hands, something about his look made me feel like he wasn't happy about his win. It was like he didn't like beating me like that. We became friends soon after."

"He wasn't a guy that people liked right off the bat. As a matter fact, he probably pissed off more people than not. In our match, he had this passionate look in eyes, like he was in love with playing golf. If you didn't pay attention you would miss it. If you didn't understand that look, he wouldn't just beat you, he would embarrass you."

"Later, I asked him about it, and he told me that so many guys have a little talent and only care about winning. They have no love for the game. They only care about the power it gives them. He said those guys strip the game of its beauty. He hated those people and made it well known when they played. I've been in a group with him when some arrogant bastard's down a couple grand and pressing every bet on sixteen.

Six bets, all worth about four hundred a pop, and he birdies two of the last three holes. By now, this guy is pissed. He has a two-footer to tie the hole and like four presses and he makes him putt it. The guy starts bitching and Hunter tells him to pay half of what he'll lose on a miss and he'll let it go."

"He was taunting him, and it was working. He'd say things like 'there is no way you are going to make that putt' or 'you're so scared, if you started pissin' right now, you'd miss your pants.' I'll be damned if the guy didn't miss. I asked him later why he did all that.

"Hunter said, 'Fuck him,' and that the guy had no passion for the game, no love. It was just about power to him. So, I took away the power he wanted, so badly. You see, his fear was not just losing, it was about looking weak. That's what made that putt the longest two feet he had ever seen. Hunter said he wanted to play that guy every day till he broke. Then maybe, he could feel what the game has to offer, the love it gives us when we get out of the way."

"I knew that day, what Hunter was really all about. I knew I would always be his friend." Mike leaned back and took a long drink.

I sat there and thought of Saul. I knew exactly who he was talking about and he was right. Saul was all about the love of golf.

"Wow," I said. "I would've loved to see that. I think I would have liked your friend." Mike just nodded.

We had another beer and talked golf. Nothing more said about what he wanted to know. After a bit, I got up to say goodnight.

"You know," I said, "you can see some great games

at CCNC when you watch from a distance through some binoculars. You might just see what you've been missing all this time."

"Is that so, Blu?"

"I'd stay a hole or two away, in the trees. They sell binoculars in the pro shop." I turned and left.

The next morning, I woke up early. I was excited for the match we had been working on for the last year. I mean, I wasn't just excited, I was giddy. To me, it was just such an odd occurrence. Neither of the guys were exceptionally great golfers, but still, the match had an irresistible intrigue to it. The year-long buildup must have really sucked me in.

I went to the club alone to eat and get ready. Rich was already standing by the bag drop when I arrived. He watched me pull up and I walked over to him.

"Hey, Blu," he said.

I waved; small talk wasn't on the menu.

"It's probably not smart to go anywhere alone for the next few days," he said. "If you're not with Dom, find me and I'll go with you."

I nodded. I am sure he could see I wasn't happy about it.

"You're carrying right?"

"Yes," I said.

"Did you load it?" His smile grew when he saw my face. He knew the answer was no.

"Didn't think I needed to."

"Well, it's kind of important to the whole deal." He teased.

I called him a smart ass and asked if he wanted to have breakfast. He declined and I went inside.

Sitting at the table, waiting on my food, I realized that the opportunity to run may never show itself. I might have to make an opportunity. That would mean the decision has to be made first, instead of waiting around for an out. I also realized that making that decision right now had serious consequences. It would be considered premeditation to Dom and Saul, a lack of trust. It would be a definite betrayal, one that our friendship would not survive.

Halfway through my breakfast, Mike walked in with Woody. When they sat down, they waved me over. I put up a finger and pointed to my plate indicating I would be there after I finished eating. The night before, Mike had asked me to get a caddie for Woody and I arranged for a guy named Walter to be on his bag.

I dropped a tip on the table, picked up my coffee, and went to sit down with them.

"Blu, I'm shocked to see you here," said Woody.

"Why is that? You know I live here, and you know I'm a caddie. A match like this between two whales, shit, every caddie I know wanted this loop."

"I mean, I met you at Kahkwa Club. Now, low and behold, you're here and you got this loop," Woody speculated. "Just a bit curious."

"Well," I began, "if you like that, you're going to

love that Mike asked me to get you a caddie. His name is Walter. He's a good caddie and a real good player."

"You're not setting me up with a guy to help Dom win, are ya?"

"Woody, I'm gonna let that go and chalk it up to you not knowing me," I said. I was annoyed, but I kept that to myself. "Just so you understand, I wouldn't be okay seeing something like that happen; much less, being a part of it. Anyone who would do something like that should be banished from the game; can't even hold a club in their hands at a driving range. That's a damn disgrace."

Mike smiled when I said that.

Woody said to him, "Hey Mikey, he sounds just like someone we used to know, doesn't he?"

Still smiling, Mike looked right at me. "Sure does. Sounds just like him," he said, drawing out each word. I had no intention of ever letting anyone know that I had put it all together, but Mike knew I had. I liked Mike and I knew he loved Saul. Part of me was happy he knew. A pleasant smile came across his face and stayed there.

I was so caught up talking to them that I hadn't noticed the two guys sitting across the room, conspicuously drinking their coffee in silence. I had never seen them before, so I knew they weren't members. By the way they were dressed, they weren't even golfers. Around the third time they looked over at us, I got up without saying a word to Mike or Woody and walked out to find Rich.

He was still at the bag drop. I nodded my head off to the side when he saw me so we could talk privately. He nodded back and walked around the corner after me. Despite the frequent tension, it was getting easier to work with Rich.

"I am guessing that you're who to talk to if I see something off." He smiled.

"Like the two guys in the grill, drinking coffee," he said, "or the car in the parking lot with a guy who's been sitting in it, twiddling his thumbs for the last hour? Or did you notice the three new guys on the greens crew, two of whom have never cut a blade of grass or dug a hole in their life? You mean that kind of *off*? Yeah, I'm the guy." I was listening and looking over his shoulder for the car he mentioned, at the same time.

There it was. And it did look out of place. I didn't see the greens crew, but I'm sure he was right.

"Okay, good to know," I said. I turned to walk away, but he caught my arm.

Rich explained, "Blu, the guys in the grill are with us and so are the three on the greens crew." That was a relief, well, sort of. He went on, "I have no idea who is in that car, though. I will soon. And you were right. If you see something, tell me right away. Now, Blu, go load that piece now, will ya? This isn't the time to argue. This is the time for staying alive, alright?"

I nodded. "Yeah. I got it, Rich."

I don't know if I felt safer or not. Rich seemed to be way over-prepared. Either that or I was just completely naive about what was coming. Either way, I was now officially worried. It is one thing to know that danger may be in the future and put the thought away. It's another thing to be suddenly faced with the specific type of danger and have to figure out how to react. I was scared. Knowing it's a present threat, but not necessarily immediate, was way worse.

This was throwing me way off my game. I suddenly understood the term 'head on a swivel' that I'd heard in war movies. I was looking at everything so fast, from one person to the next. I felt like drug mule going through customs. It's safe to say I did *not* like this feeling.

I went to the locker room and sat in one of the stalls, trying to breathe in hopes of regaining my composure. After about ten minutes, I heard someone walk in and stop at the sinks. Then, instead of hearing water, nothing. It felt like he was waiting for me. After a couple minutes I heard a man's voice break the silence.

"Blu, you cannot do this shit." It was Rich.

I got up and left the stall to see him leaning against the sinks. He stood up, walked towards me, and grabbed my shoulders. "You have got to pull yourself together," he said. "Shit is happening and there is nothing we can do to stop it. All we can do is plan to come out alive. Blu, you start acting all spastic, you're gonna get yourself shot. The players in this are all playing to win, and they can't have any wildcards pop up. When they see someone acting like you are right now, they'll kill you just to maintain mission integrity."

I nodded. "I understand," I said, "just give me a minute." He left after giving me a once-over. I splashed some water on my face. I mumbled to my reflection in the mirror.

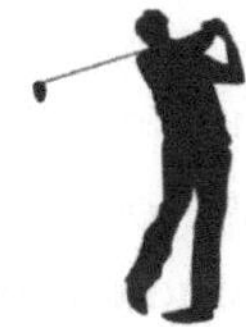

CHAPTER 14

"Blu get your shit together," I told myself. "If today's the last day, be okay with that. Don't act like a bitch in the end."

I finally knew the answer to Dom's question. I closed my eyes and recited Mr. Graham's prayer. I'd read it every night since Saul gave it to me. When I finished, I pulled out the paper and wrote the date under where Saul had written his. I chuckled as I slid it back in my wallet. It must look like I'm grasping at straws to save myself. First Saul, then Dom, then the lifestyle. And now, God. This time felt different, though. I felt this strange calm come over me. At that moment, I knew Steve and Saul were right. I wasn't as worried anymore. If this was to be my last day, I'd make it a good one.

Don't get me wrong. I was still on edge, but I wasn't shaking in my boots. I felt more prepared, ready to act if I had to. Looking in the mirror, I was barely recognizable from the guy who first met Saul, a year ago.

When I walked out to get Dom's bag from the guys in the bag room, I looked at every person. Not just looked at them, I studied them. I knew there was no way I could live like this forever, but for now, I concentrated on getting through the day. Funny thing, when faced with a situation like this, you have no long-term plans anymore. At least I didn't.

Dom walked up and put his hand on my shoulder like he had before. "Stop thinking," he said.

I nodded and he went on.

"Blu just go about your job. If the time comes to act, if you are lucky enough to see it beforehand, it will all move in slow motion. You will have plenty of time to act. And if you don't see it beforehand, it won't matter." He started laughing and it made me smile. I felt safe around Dom. Not sure why, exactly. I just did.

We went to the range and to the short game green and, lastly, we hit some putts. Dom was focused and ready. I could see he was a totally different person when getting ready to compete. He was in game mode.

He had seen Woody and Mike and said hi to Mike, but nothing at all to Woody. Dom wanted to win this, and I sensed it had more to do with winning in general than with beating Woody. He didn't have a look of hate on his face. It was more like a competitive fire that burned from within.

At the first tee, I was given the task of presenting the opening rules and instructions. I set the bag by the side of the tee and got started.

"Gentlemen," I announced, "if you could come listen so I may welcome you to this event and state the rules of the match, I would appreciate it."

They both stepped up and I continued.

"This will be a two-day, thirty-six-hole, stroke play event. It will be played on both the Dogwood and Cardinal courses, here at CCNC. Local rules apply; you can find those on the back of the scorecard. The greens crew has been kind enough to mark both courses for all hazards and any ground under repair. If it isn't marked off, play it. In the event of a tie, a sudden death playoff will begin ten minutes after completion of the thirty-sixth hole and will start on number ten of the Cardinal course. Please identify your golf balls and I wish both of you gentlemen good luck. Mr. Woodworth, you will tee first."

I looked around and it was only us four on the tee. I wondered where Mike was. I didn't see him anywhere. On the third hole, I finally spotted him, way up by the green, off in the trees, looking through his binoculars at the action. Just as I looked away, something caught my eye. Another figure walked up from behind him and stopped. No one else would have known, but after seeing him every day for a year, I knew it was Saul. I smiled for a second, then I started looking around. I was worried that someone else might see them. They spoke for a few minutes and then hugged. Then, Saul was gone.

The match was boring, through four; all even and all pars with no birdie scares. Each one was waiting for the other to make a mistake. Neither were taking any chances.

On the fifth hole, things changed. Woody pulled his drive left and it ended up next to a tree leaving him with a punch out to the first cut of rough as his only option. Emboldened by this, Dom hit his drive right down the middle and his approach landed within three feet of a pin that was tucked right behind a trap. I told him the smart play was the center of the green to guarantee a one-shot lead with a par. Dom nodded.

"But a birdie will take the wind out of him," he said, deviously, "and we could have him beat by nine." That was Dom, a competitor to the end. He was not nervous at all. He was one of those guys that thrive in the clutch. They enjoy it so much that it never occurred to them to be nervous.

Saul and I were talking once about the different types of competitors, their personalities, and how some guys are better at handling pressure. He told me about how he got nervous when he was younger until one day when it dawned on him. In tough situations, or at the end of a game when you have a chance to win, people tend to get nervous. He said that's why we play, to get in that type of situation. So, why get nervous and ruin it? You may win, you may lose, but whatever you do, don't ruin by getting nervous.

The course today was calm. We sailed through the first five holes and didn't see another soul. Woody was still one over and Dom, one under. The sixth hole was a long par four. I handed Dom his driver.

"Swing within yourself, solid in the middle, that's all you need."

For the second time today, he didn't listen. He really went after it, trying to shorten the hardest hole on the course and it didn't work out the way he'd intended. From the tee, it went well right into the trees. He could, maybe, advance it enough to get to the green in three. Woody was down the middle, but he didn't hit it well at all. It was safe, but a long way out.

Dom's ball was not in great shape. It was far back from the green, so that didn't really matter cause even in the fairway he couldn't reach the green. He asked for his four iron and as I handed it to him, then he asked me my thoughts.

"Hold the club tight," I told him, "take it outside and come down sharply on the ball. All you want to do is get it slicing hard and rolling down the fairway. And when I say down sharply, don't think hard, but real solid. Make sure it starts left of that tree." I pointed to a giant pine tree about twenty feet ahead of him.

He asked about hitting it further to the right, through a gap it the trees. I shook my head.

"Dom," I said. "That would be the stupidest shot you could possibly hit. This is a thirty-six-hole match, don't lose the match with a nine, trying to hit a shot that you have little chance of pulling off."

He smiled and, thankfully, did as I told him to. He hit a better shot than I thought he would. It rolled down the fairway to about a hundred and seventy yards out. Woody hit his fairway metal and really caught it. He was on the left side, just short of the green by about forty yards.

I was starting to understand what Saul had meant when he said Woody was clueless about playing a course. I mean, if you can't get it to the green, at least leave yourself a full swing and not some half-wedge that with a lot of feel to it. You could pull it off if you were a tour player, but he's a four handicap. Attempting a half-wedge to the green is not the highest percentage shot in your bag.

True to form, he chunked it and left it on the front of the green about forty feet away for par. Dom had a twenty-footer for par. They both two putted for bogey. The match stayed with Dom two up through fourteen holes.

Then, on fifteen, things changed. On this course, hole 15 is a par five that is reachable in two *if* you hit a good drive. I mean, a real good drive. Dom knew it and he really went after his drive; put it right in the woods. I told him to hit another, but he was pissed.

"We'll find it."

Woody was in the center of the fairway in a good position and might be able to get home in two. As I thought, we couldn't find Dom's ball and he had to walk back to the tee to hit his third shot. He was getting tired and the extra walking along with the anger did not help.

Woody hit his next as Dom walked back and was twenty yards away from the green. Pretty good shape. Dom's third shot from the tee went down the left side in the high rough. He got his fourth shot out in the fairway but a long way from the green. He hit a four iron and caught it heavy in the front trap.

Woody hit his approach shot to three feet and putted out for birdie. He was even, now. Dom's trap shot ended up eight feet away, but he missed it. Tapping in for a triple bogey eight. He was now two down at two over par.

They both made par on the next two holes and Woody's second shot was right on target on eighteen. It was going to be close. That's when the golf gods took control. His ball hit the pin near the base and ricocheted into the greenside bunker. From there, he'd never get it up and down in two. He settled for a bogey.

Dom, on the other hand, made a twenty-footer for birdie to get the match back to even at the halfway point. Dom was excited about the turn of events and displayed his usual smile that hadn't been present for the last four hours. When he competed, he was serious.

I could see he wasn't just a good player; he really loved the game.

I wiped the clubs down at the bag drop. Dom came back from the rest room just as I finished.

"That was a lot of nothing. Surrounded by some crazy-ass golf, wouldn't you say, Blu?" he joked.

I laughed in agreement. He asked if I was ready to go and we made our way to the parking lot. We stepped off of the curb and saw a man leaning on the side of Dom's car, looking down at his phone. When he lifted his head, I recognized him. It was Vincent, from the Speakeasy in Sanford. Dom froze for a second. Then, he told me to go grab the clubs. I did and, when I returned, Dom was still there, maybe fifty yards from his car with Vincent still leaning on it.

"Just stay behind me. I'll handle this," he said.

He walked to his car and I put the bag back down. Vincent stood up and greeted Dom with a smile, saying, "Hey there."

Dom started right in on him. "You mother-fucking wop. What the fuck are you doing here?"

"I needed to make sure there weren't no fuck ups on this thing," Vincent squared off with Dom. "Oh, and I heard a rumor that you put a hit out on me," he pointed at Dom and put a hand on his chest. "But I said no, no way, not my Dominic. He would *never* do that. I came down here to verify that fact. Tell me. Am I right?"

"Get your facts straight," Dom said. "You only know half of it. I *did* put a hit on you, contingent on me being dead on Tuesday. If I stay alive, there is no hit. That's my way of keeping you to your word. Besides, do you really think you heard about it by chance? You think some guy that works for me ran his mouth? I made sure you knew about it."

"If I were you, I would get the fuck out of here and meet Kenny on Monday. Do what he says, so you don't fuck this thing up. I did time once and I won't do it again for you, never again."

They stared each other down until Vincent blinked.

"Okay Dom, I'll do what Kenny tells me to do, but don't fuck this up. I will fucking kill you and everybody you know if you do." Dom nodded as Vincent turned to walk away.

Dom told me to go get Woody and Rich, so I set his clubs down by the rear of his car and quickly went back to the pro shop. I saw Rich and told him to go to the parking lot to see Dom. I found Woody walking out of the men's room and I told him that Dom needed to see him in the parking lot.

When we got to Dom, he was leaning against his car.

"Nice day," he said to Woody. "You played well."

"You, too, Dominic," Woody replied. "And it's good to see you. When this is over, we should talk about some things."

"You're probably right," said Dom, "but for now we need to move tomorrow's round. Don't ask me why, we just do. I will get us a course for the day, just don't leave the gates until morning. Rich will pick you up at 8am, sharp." He waited for a nod from Woody.

"Woody, please tell Mike. Do exactly what I told you and everything will be fine. I want to make damn sure of it. The new course will be one that neither of us have played and I'll make sure we have two caddies that have, okay?"

"Sounds good, Dom." Woody agreed.

We parted ways and drove to the house. On the way, Dom called Saul to fill him in and ask him to arrange a new course.

"Yeah, I know. Saul, this is what I need. Whatever the cost, the course needs to be closed." There was a pause, "Yeah, completely closed," and another pause, "I'll pay extra. That includes the greens crews being gone by nine, right? Can you do that? Okay, good. We'll talk in a bit."

I arrived at the house, grabbed a beer, and went down to the game room to shoot some pool. His house was a pretty standard 1980's build; not big, but plenty of room. It had a basement that was nice, but also kind of weird. When you went downstairs, at the bottom of the landing and through a doorway, there was a nice sized game room with a 9-foot pool table and a card table in the corner. In the back was a tavern like bar where a bartender could walk behind to make drinks and people could sit, facing him. There were three flat screen TVs on the wall. Weirdly, there were no windows and if, or when, you closed the door to the stairs, you could see the door for what it was. It was a foot thick and made of steel, heavy. The lock on the inside was a big wheel like you'd see on a safe or a ship. That's when it would click. You were in a really nice panic room.

I was in there playing pool for about half an hour before Saul walked in with Dom and Mike. I greeted Mike and they got out sticks. We played scotch doubles for the next two hours. During that time, I found out we'd be playing the second round of the match at Tobacco Road. There was only going to be one person in the shop and no one else. No one else on the property, at all. I just shook my head when I heard that. I said Goodnight just after nine and went to bed.

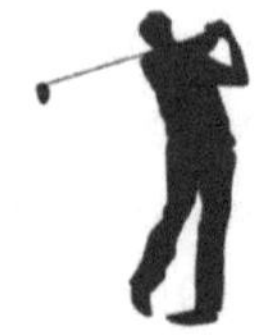

CHAPTER 15

I woke up around 6am and went down to make coffee, but I could smell that someone already had. Mike and Saul were already chatting on the back deck. They were in good spirits and laughed together as they caught up. I said, "Good morning," and decided to go make breakfast so they could continue their conversation.

By eight, Dom was downstairs. He was already dressed and ready to go. I made a breakfast shake and grabbed some of the bacon they had cooked for everyone. He didn't say much. He just got in the car when we were all ready.

It was a forty-minute drive up to the Tobacco Road Golf Club and I was looking forward to it. It was a Mike

Strantz design and a beast, although it was only like 6,700 yards long. It was target golf with some unusual twists. There were no sand traps and no rakes. The only sand was a waste bunker and if you were in one you could pick up your ball, smooth the sand and replace it before you hit. The reason was so that you could, and would, drive carts in them if you took a cart. Approach shots were so different from huge swales in the greens. And they were fast. If you used a Stimpmeter to measure the speed of the green, it would roll an 11, every day. Let me tell you, an 11 is very fast. That speed will only lend itself to those with real skill in their short game.

It was a wonderful course. I loved it. Dom had never played it although we spoke about it a lot. We kept intending to play it, but before we knew it, a year had passed.

To his credit, Strantz kept it pretty natural, using the non-golf-like terrain in the design. That's was what made it both unique and exciting to play at the same time. It's well known that Strantz was a Dead Head and there is little doubt in my mind that he was on acid when he designed that course. His unique vision for raw terrain was unparalleled by any other designers to date. Today was going to be fun.

Because Woody's first caddie, Walter, had never seen this course before, I arranged for another guy named Jamie Whitley to carry for him, today. Jamie was a good caddie and a really good player.

Tobacco Road's clubhouse was a small old house

that was redone when they built the course. There was nothing special going on except for great golf. That's what Tobacco Road was all about.

When we got to the pro shop, we were told that Woody and his caddie were already on the range.

"Mr. Ciacchini," said the guy behind the counter, "if that's all you will need from me, I will be leaving as soon as you tee off. There will be a cooler with snacks and refreshments on the tee, every four holes. I will leave the clubhouse unlocked. Feel free to use it for as long as you want. I only ask that someone call me when you leave."

With that, he handed Dom a paper. I assumed had his number on it. "I will call when we leave," said Dom as he gave the man a few rooled up one hundred dollar bills. Dom passed the paper to me and we left. We went to the first tee to warm up and I addressed the players again.

"Gentlemen, these are the last eighteen holes of the match. Just as yesterday, the course is marked, and local rules are on the scorecard. There are no sand traps and no rakes. If you are in a waste bunker, you may lift the ball and smooth the sand, then replace the ball and hit away.

"Players, if there are no questions, please identify the balls you will be playing." They did and I said, "Mr. Ciacchini, you have the tee. Good luck, gentlemen." Dom bent over to place his tee and everyone else backed off.

I won't walk you through all eighteen holes because, honestly, there are only four that stick out. Dom and Woody each had-two birdies and two bogies from the other fourteen holes. Woody's bogies were three putts and Dom's were from missing the green and not getting up and down. The birdies for each were plain: hit it close and make a putt. Nothing all too thrilling. But the other four, well, they were something.

The first hole was a par five and kind of funky. The fairway ran beside the tenth hole with the tee about ninety yards above the fairway. The fairway was bordered by a hill on either side, covered in high grass and blackberry vines. There were vines everywhere on this course. It made looking for errant shots a real commitment on the part of those who chose to do so.

I have seen many golfers come out of those woods with cuts all over their legs after looking for a ball. It was why I had a first aid kit packed in the bag. I knew, playing golf here was like playing a pickup football game when I was young: someone would leaving bleeding.

Dom's shot was in the center of the fairway. It was a good drive, but not very long. Woody, on the other hand, was fifty yards past Dom, on the left side. He cleared the hill and had about two hundred and thirty yards to the hole with a great angle to a back right pin. Dom laid up short of a waste area that crossed the fairway.

Woody, all 'Woody-like', hit a three metal and then, unlike himself, hit it at the right side of a hidden green.

We couldn't see it land but he was either very close or in the waste area to the right of the green. The green sloped front to back and right to left with a big camelback in the middle of the green.

When we got over the waste area that Dom laid up short of, we could see that Woody was close, real close, like five feet past the hole and inside ten feet away. Dom hit a wedge, about fifteen feet above and right of the hole; not the best location. He pushed the shot a little right of where he wanted to be, and it cost him. His putt wasn't an easy one and he missed it, letting it roll five feet past the hole. He opted to putt out and made par.

Woody lined up his putt, taking his time, which was not his norm in stressful situations. Because he did, he made it for eagle. Woody was now two up and still two up on the sixteenth tee.

Now, the sixteenth hole was a unique tee. The hole travels upward over tall grass in a waste area. You couldn't see the fairway from the tee and your target was a steam pipe made into a bird feeder that was placed on the far side of the fairway. Both sides of the fairway gave way to a waste area on a hillside.

From the fairway, the hole traveled uphill and left to a green that was maybe fifty feet above the fairway. It sloped back to front with several swales in it along with a small camelback mound in the center.

Woody hit the fairway and Dom was in the waste area. Dom couldn't do anything but punch out towards the fairway. Woody hit the left side of the green, maybe twenty-five feet away, but this did not leave him an easy putt. Dom was a little aggravated and hit a wedge long and right of the green. Although he was off the green, he was closer than Woody.

So, Woody putted up about five feet below the hole. Dom had a real hard shot downhill, without much green to work with. He hit his lob wedge and it landed about three feet away, slowly picking up pace as it approached the hole. I was praying for it to slow down. He can't go down four with a double bogey here. The ball started turning left and was going faster than I wanted it to. He was going to be about twenty feet away for bogey when it stopped if it stopped. If it didn't stop, who knows how far the putt would be.

A poorly repaired ball mark bounced the ball to the right, and it hit the base of the pin and fell in. Dom cried, "Hell yeah, baby!" and I jumped in the air. Being unprepared, I landed like Phil Michelson at the Masters. His was the worst victory jump ever, but mine was a good second. Woody just shook his head at Jamie, the caddie.

We arrived to the seventeenth with Dom, two down. Seventeen was a real strange hole. The green was about ninety feet below the tee and although it was just under a hundred and sixty yards it played like less. The green was, maybe, a hundred and twenty feet from left to right. It was cut into two sections on its right and left by a mound in the center that ran from front to back. That was about nine feet in height. The pin was on the left and that brought the waste area that surrounded the left side and front of the green into play.

Woody hit safely on the left fringe and, although it usually rolls off the fringe towards the hole due to the slope and speed of the greens, his held up in the fringe. Now, it was Dom's turn to hit and he took a nine iron and pushed it towards the center of the mound, well right of the pin. I was hoping it would land far enough left of the center of the mound that it would roll down to a flatter portion of the green. It hit the mound dead center, maybe thirty feet right of the hole, and with one bounce, it stopped. I cursed under my breath and grabbed Dom's nine iron from him and started walking towards the green.

I took two steps and looked back again at the green. Dom's ball was starting to roll, ever so slightly, to the left, towards the hole. I stopped and put my hand on Dom's shoulder. He turned and I pointed at the green. Slowly, it picked up pace. Woody and Jamie had stopped to watch. All four of us were standing in silence, staring as it rolled faster. It lost momentum as it got to the flat section where the hole was, but it still had a fair amount of speed. "Slow down," I said, to no one in particular as the ball approached the hole.

Bam! Just like that, it was gone. Dom looked at me, stunned. "You have got to be fucking kidding me," Woody exclaimed. Dom smiled as he slowly turned to Woody.

"If you miss, we're even," Dom said. He laughed out

loud. He was walking on a cloud and I was smiling but keeping a lot inside as to show Woody and the match some respect. Woody two putted, lipping out on the first putt.

The match was down to the last hole. It was hole, number thirty-six in the match, the eighteenth of the day. The players and their caddies talked in hushed tones. It was time to be serious and everyone knew it.

Dom, still on high from the ace, hit a drive to the right side that drew back to the center. He didn't swing all that hard, but he really caught this one. Woody took a good swing at it and hit it solid but left in the trees, he couldn't hit the green without hooking his shot hard.

When we got to the balls, it was obvious that Woody was not in great shape. He went first and, hooding the club, managed to connect with a hard hook that actually curved too far and left him it the waste area just short and left of the green. Dom hit a nine iron that stopped the ball where it landed, eight feet right of the hole.

Woody's pitch shot landed and rolled about eighteen feet short of the hole. Woody took his time and hit a great putt that went in the right center of the cup. That left Dom with an eight-foot putt to win it all. He settled into his routine and took his time to look at the break from both sides of the hole. He looked at me and I nodded.

"Three inches outside, right? What do you think?" I said to him.

"Yeah," Dom agreed, "I think so."

Dom stepped up, looking down the line twice this time. Dom stood up as Woody walked into his line of sight.

"It's good," said Woody. His tone and demeanor told me he was conceding on not just the putt, but the match as well.

"The hell it is," Dominic declared. "I'm putting it."

Woody walked up close to Dom and said, "Chris told me everything."

Dom replied. "He should not have done that."

"Why not," Woody said, "it could have saved us from years of bad blood. Why didn't you tell me yourself?"

I was completely lost. I didn't understand what they were talking about. I just stood there, watching. Later that night, Mike said Woody told him the following:

"Woody's wife was leaving the club and Chris, Woody's son, was driving his mother home because she'd had too much to drink. She didn't know that Chris happened to be at Dom's house drinking with his friend, Anthony, who was Dom's son, and Tom another friend. Well, Chris's mother called him for a ride, and he went to get her at the Club. It's only a five-mile drive but, on the way home, a car swerved and almost hit them. It forced Chris off the road, and they hit a tree. His mother, Woody's wife, was killed in the accident. It was a desolated road and the first person to drive up was Dom. He realized that Chris was drunk and called

Anthony to come and take Chris to the house. He told him to bring Tom to drive his car home.

Before he left, Dom told Anthony to hit Chris so that it looked like they'd been in a fight. It was a way to explain Chris's injuries to anyone that might ask. He also told them both to say they were at the house all night and to never say anything different, no matter what happens.

Anthony drove Chris to the Ciacchini house. Dom took a sharp piece of metal that fell from the car and cut his face. He dialed 911 and, when the cops showed up, it looked like Dom was driving and had lost control of the car. By doing this, Dom saved Chris's life from ruin. Almost consequently though, he destroyed a friendship. Woody, along with everyone else, wondered why Dom and Woody's wife were together. An affair was assumed, which caused the long rift between the two men. Dom never told anyone what happened, including and especially Woody.

The answer to why he didn't tell anyone was typical Dom. "Want to keep something secret?" he said, "tell no one."

When Woody asked, Dom answered, "I wasn't going to see your son's life ruined over this. We could have saved our friendship, but it wasn't worth compromising Chris's future. Even if he got off of any and all charges, this is a small town. This is our town and this sort of thing would stay with him forever; haunt him. He was a kid. One of *our* kids and I wanted, as I know you would, the very best for him. You were about to have enough on your plate, raising two teenagers all alone. Just being without her. You didn't need anything more. So, I took the hit."

Woody looked stunned. He wrapped his arms around Dom and began thanking him over and over again. I saw a side of Dom that really impressed me as I listened to his story. It made me feel proud to tell people that he and I are friends.

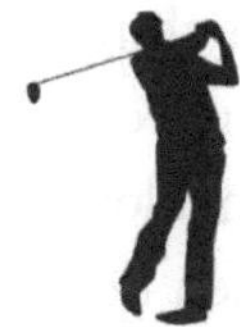

CHAPTER 16

That next morning, I was sitting at Pine Needles, waiting on Dom and Saul. We had not been to Pine Needles since after the Charlotte trip. The trip that left them wanting more security and control of their surroundings. They needed a gated community, like CCNC, where the guards could call if anyone came looking. But, that's just conjecture on my part.

"Pretty day huh, Blu?" It was Saul speaking. "I love a golf course in the morning; so peaceful. It makes you think about the day to come and all the possibilities that lay ahead." He stretched. "Makes an old man feel young."

"It is nice, Boss," I said. "Real nice." I smiled, feeling a little younger myself. Dom walked down from the clubhouse. I turned to wave and saw Rich exiting the clubhouse with two caddies behind him. Jamie, who was on Woody's bag yesterday, was one of them. He hit his vape a couple of times before they got close. That vape pipe had something strong in it and it wasn't flavored water. It made me chuckle. I didn't care a bit. I liked Jamie, I liked him a lot, actually. He was mellow and fun to talk to. When he got to where we were, he reached out to shake my hand.

"Hello, sir," he said as we shook hands. "I'm Jamie and I'll be your caddie today. If there is anything you need, just let me know."

I laughed. "Jamie, one thing I do need is for you to just call me Blu. We're friends and I'm just a caddie like you that a got a real good loop. Went more than 18.."

"I'd say so," he said. "You know where I can get another one of those?" Everybody laughed.

"Let's go," said Saul. "We're playing today, and our tee time is coming up." We walked to the first tee.

As we were getting our gloves and balls out. I put my wallet and watch in the bag. I looked over and saw Rich doing the same thing, except true to form, with guns. For the last year, I've watched him tote around not one, but three damn guns in his bag. He pulled one out of his belt line from behind his back, another from his hip pocket, and the third from a holster on his right ankle.

Rich never tried to conceal what he was doing. To him, it was a normal thing to store a mobile arsenal in a golf bag. It was nothing less than perfect. I shook my head as I looked at Jamie, who was trying hard to not burst with laughter.

It was a nice day and, at first, I wasn't happy that Rich was there. It was likely just old jealousy rearing its head. It went away quickly, though, as Saul walked and talked with me alone for most of the round. We laughed a lot. It was nice to spend time with him, one on one, like this. Dom and Rich spent most of the round talking only to each other. They always looked serious, like they were talking business the entire time, except for the cordial small talk they offered on the green.

After teeing off on the eighteenth fairway, Saul stopped me. He signaled to Jamie to keep walking towards the balls in the fairway.

"Blu," Saul said. "I want you know how much I appreciate your friendship and that the times we've spent together have been times I'll never forget. I hope you don't forget, either. Please remember it all and pass it along."

I tilted my head. "You're talking like you're going to die."

He just smiled. "We're are all dying, Blu. Each one of us is alone, coming and going. It's just nice to find people you like to share the time in between with." I didn't have a clue where he was going with this.

We hit our approach shots, but I was really paying more attention to Saul than my shot. When we got to the green, Jamie gave me a read, "Two cups, outside right. Don't think, just hit it there." He pointed to the spot where he wanted me to aim.

I noticed that everyone had gone quiet, now focused on the putt. I looked at Saul and tilted my head, not understanding what was going on with them. Finally, Saul spoke.

"You have no idea where you're at right now, do you?"

I straightened up.

"All day, you've been so wrapped up in our conversations that you played this whole round how real players play golf. You thought of nothing other than the next shot and, after each hit, forgot all about it. That's how real golf is played, one shot at a time. Here you are, blissfully unaware of where you are, score-wise."

Then it suddenly occurred to me, like a bolt of lightning. I had made seven birdies, no bogies. If I make this, I'm at sixty-four. Sixty-fucking-four. You've got to be kidding me. Saul spoke softer now.

"Blu just hit the putt where he pointed. Nothing else matters. If it goes in or not, all you can control is hitting that ball to that target. Not a thing else matters. You'll leave here today having shot a good round of golf, either way." Saul paused for a moment and then went on. "Remember this morning, how calm it was? That calm came from inside of you, not the other way around. Let it come out, now."

I thought about it and noticed the feeling he spoke

of, swelling up inside of me. It washed over my being. He was right. I felt so at peace as I stepped up to the putt. I fixed my eyes on my spot and swung the putter effortlessly. The ball rolled like it was drawn to the cup; like they belonged together. Everything happened so slowly. Just as the ball ran out of speed, it fell into the hole.

It seemed so surreal. I was overwhelmed with this new level of calm. It was, for lack of a better description, beautiful. I stood there, gazing at the hole as I wafted back into reality. Dom and Rich were cheering. I broke out into a huge smile as Jamie grabbed the ball from the hole and threw it to me. I looked at Saul and realized that I finally understood everything he'd been telling me this whole last year. The idea of energy and connection and getting out of my own way.

We walked down to the putting green. Saul lead the way.

"Damn good round, Blaise," he said.

I looked at him, confused. "Not Blu?"

"Not today, Mr. Jones, not after that round."

I smiled. Saul asked me and Rich to go to the range for a minute to give himself and Dom a chance to talk. At the range, Rich took out a club but never got to up hit. I heard a noise from the direction of the clubhouse and then I saw them.

Kenny, Vincent, and someone else I didn't know were walking up. I stopped and grabbed the gun from my bag. Rich just kept staring at the two of them talking on the green. I told Rich I was going to the shop to get a new glove. He just nodded. I walked around the side of the building and through the parking lot. My plan, although not entirely thought through, was to come up behind them and stop them from doing whatever they were about to do. If I was right, they were here to kill Saul.

I walked through the parking lot and saw Steve sitting in the back seat of a car. I assumed, from the way he sat, that he was tied up. I made eye contact and he motioned his head in the direction of where they were. I ran to where I had last seen them and, like an unexpected firework show, a gun shot rang out. Then another shot. It echoed across the parking lot. Two more followed, but from farther away.

I rounded the corner and came to a stumbling halt. It took a second to comprehend what I was seeing. Vincent was on the ground, bleeding from his chest. Kenny was kneeling next to him wiping off his gun. He put it in Vincent's hand and pressed Vince's fingers against the metal. Then, he let his hand and the gun fall to the ground next to him. The third guy, with Kenny, hadn't seen me, yet. He lifted his gun and aimed it at Kenny. He spoke, "Two down, two to go." Before I could even think, his gunshot filled my ears and there was buzzing in my head. As I blinked the blur from my eyes, I saw Kenny looking at me with a smile. The other guy was on the ground, bleeding.

There was smoke coming from the barrel of the gun

I held. Kenny walked up to me and put his hand over my hand, grabbing the gun.

"Blu, you okay?" I said nothing. "I'm gonna need this back, okay?" I just stared at him. He took the gun from my hand and pushed my arm down to my side. "Find Rich," he ordered. "I need to get this out of here."

I nodded. It was more of an instinct than a conscious decision. He stood directly in front of me as he spoke. "You were on the range the whole time. Rich will tell you what to say. Go now." I started to walk to the range. I was in a dream. Then, I heard Kenny yell, "Blu, get your ass moving! This aint a fucking game!" I started running.

I rounded the corner and saw Rich holding a gun. Then I saw Saul lying on the green. I tried running over to him, but Dom stopped me, wrapping his arms around me like a bear hug.

"He's gone, Blu," Dom whispered.

"Wait. What?" I was spinning.

"He's gone, he's down," Dom repeated. "Everything's going to be alright. Just go back to Rich. Just go, Blu. It will be okay." Tears were blanketing my face as I ran to the range where Rich was still standing, gun in hand.

We all waited in silence as we heard the sirens coming closer. Two cops came walking down, through the trees, guns drawn, but something was off. Another guy was with them. He was following the cops and his identification badge said he was a medical examiner.

I had to force my way through the fog in my head to process everything in that moment.

The cops and the examiner stopped and spoke with Dom, first. Dom pointed at Saul, then at the other guy dead on the hill, and then to Rich as he spoke. The cops looked at Saul, blood seeping steadily into his shirt. They spoke to the examiner, briefly, before walking over to the other body. The examiner put Saul in a body bag, zipped it almost all the way up, and had him in the van in no time. The cops continued to inspect the other body. Rich was standing next to me and turned to put his arms around me.

"Don't worry, Blu. It's all going to be alright," he whispered in my ear. "S'all good, right? Yeah?" He pulled away and smiled at me.

I had no idea what he meant by that and it left me more confused than I already was. Rich walked over and gave his statement to the police. Dom talked with me for a while, but I can't remember anything either of us said. The entire rest of that day and night is blank.

The next day, I got a call from a funeral home asking me to come down. When I arrived, they took me to an office and had me sign some papers before handing me an urn. It was Saul's ashes. Tears immediately flowed from my eyes.

The woman walked around from behind the desk to console me and, after some time, walked me to the door. Outside, Dom was leaning against my car. When

I got close, he stepped forward and hugged me, asking, "That's him, huh?"

I nodded. "I guess so."

Dom told me that I should spread them soon, but to pay attention when I do and to not spread them over water. He reasoned that Saul wouldn't want his last shot to land in a hazard. And then he laughed. I thought it inappropriate to laugh at a time like this, but I was too drained to give it any serious thought, let alone to say anything.

CHAPTER 17

It took me almost a week to decide how and where to spread those ashes. One morning, I woke up and I knew exactly where to put Saul. I waited till dusk that night and then walked to the eighteenth hole at Pine Needles. I emptied the urn onto the green, letting the wind carry the dust towards the fairway. A flicker of white fell to the ground. I reached down to pick it up. It was a key with a piece of paper attached. On one side, the paper read:

Blu, thank you. Always in my heart. S'all good.

And on the other side was written:

PO box 2387 SP
Check Everyday

The key looked like postal key, and I figured it was a postal key in Southern Pines. That explained the "SP" and that the note said I should check it every day. Seemed pretty straight forward.

I checked the box daily for a few weeks then one day there was a slip that said to check with the postmaster to get a package. The man handed me a pretty large box. I took it to my car and opened it. Inside were banded stacks of hundred-dollar bills. I had to look at all the stacks, to flip through each one. I thought that was strange, real strange. Total was over $200,000. A note was attached to one of the stacks. It read:

Blu,

*What a wonderful year we had. It will be
a time I will remember forever. You were
my best and maybe only true friend. Spread
the word of what you learned while we were
together. And most of all, play. You can make
a living playing this game. Just concentrate
on the next shot, only the next shot. Once you
hit, it doesn't matter where it goes.*

*See you soon.
Saul*

Also in the box was a book, titled 'The Greatest Player that Never Lived.' It was a good read. It was fictional, but I liked it. I wasn't sure why he sent it to me, but I gave up trying to figure out why Saul did anything. I miss Saul and think of him every day.

All of it seemed like a sick joke, but it *was* his handwriting. I'd seen it a hundred times. I went back to that day, wondering if there was something I missed. I saw him go down. I saw the blood. I was right there. I even shot a guy. My arms fell to my sides and I just sat there in my car, numb.

Six months after that day at Needles when he was shot, I was playing in a private tournament that I was invited to. It was one of the tournaments Saul would play in, kind of like fight club for golfers. They were all good players that loved to gamble, but nobody talked about it. If you got an invite, you brought your A game or your wallet. One bad day could lose you fifty big ones, fast. These were whales with skills.

At the end of the day, I was on the eighteenth green. From there, you could see the ninth green. I noticed a group of players farting around in the rough, and then one of the players made eye contact with me. He smiled and tipped his cap. I smiled back at him, scrambling for a clear train of thought. Could it be Saul? He had a white beard but boy it looked like him.

I was surprised, but I wasn't shocked by it after all the crazy shit I lived with for a year. Man, I did miss the crazy. Then, I thought maybe I was seeing things.

I couldn't get another look at him as they were already gone when I left the 18th green.

I looked on the tee sheet when I finished and signed my card. In his group were: Bernie DeLario, Sean Kapp, and Beau Steadman. Again, I smiled when I saw it. Beau Steadman was the main character from the book I got in that package. Yeah, *that* package. I love that book even more, now.

I left my number and address with the tournament director, along with instructions to give it to Mr. Steadman in the 11:50am group. I knew he had it already, but I hoped he would call. I trusted he knew best what to do. I wasn't going to track him down. I wasn't even sure it was him .*'See you soon.'* His words rang in my ears. And it fueled my hopes every day. I looked hoping to see him everywhere I went

I walked to my car in a daze. I was so happy to see Saul, or at least, his ghost. I was second-guessing myself, now. Above that, I won money, not just from the side bets, but since I took second overall. That was worth $7,500. A good day.

I checked my phone when I got in the car to drive home, and I had like seven missed calls from the same number. I didn't recognize the number, so I figured it was some sales call. The fact there were seven of them did make me curious, but not enough to call it, though.

An hour into a three-hour drive, I got another call. It was the same number as the seven I missed earlier, so I answered it. It was my godfather, Al Williams. I said hi and asked him why he was calling with this number. Did he get a new phone?

He interrupted me. "Blaise, we only have a minute. Listen to me. They found your friend in the back of the field. I couldn't get a hold of you. I called your friend Dominic and he called me back. I told him to get you and what it was about. I am sorry if I shouldn't have, but I did. The cops will probably want to talk to you. They were here all day and I didn't tell them anything, but who knows what they think. If you call me, call this number from some phone that's not yours or can be tied to you. My advice is to get a prepaid flip phone. Actually, get a lot of them and, if you use them, change them every week. Don't call my house or my cell. And it's probably smart if you don't call me for a while. Blaise, good luck." Then he hung up.

My mind was spinning. I wasn't sure what to do so I went through different ideas in my head for the rest of the drive. When I pulled into my driveway, something felt off. I wasn't sure what it was, but something wasn't right. When I walked through the door, I saw a guy with his back to me, sitting in my chair. I had gotten used to carrying a gun and pulled it from my belt. I was only a few paces from him when I heard a voice from the kitchen.

"He aint gonna hurt ya'."

I spun to my right and there was Rich, standing in the kitchen pointing a gun at me. He walked up to me and took my gun without any resistance on my part.

He told me to sit down. He spun the chair and I saw the guy in it was dead. Just then Kenny came up from the basement and closed the door. He nodded at Rich.

"Done," said Kenny.

Before I could speak, Rich started in. "Blu, a whole year we have been talking to you. The one thing I warned you about was leaving loose ends. Why didn't you tell me about this buddy you buried out at that farm? Nothing goes away unless you make it go away. Now you got a loose end and I can't let you become my loose end."

A set of headlights pull in the driveway. They shut off and twenty seconds later a man walks in. I recognize him as Eugene, from a pool hall in Charlotte I worked at for after graduation. But that wasn't his business. I knew he was involved in a lot of illegal stuff. I worked for him for two years after my parents died.

He walks in carrying two bags. He hands one to Rich and Rich says where is the safe. I point to the rug in the center of the room and he kicks it away. He leans over and pulls back two floorboards and exposes a safe door. Looking over to me he says Blu the combo please. I tell him and he opens the safe and starts filling the bag with the money I have in there. There was over $150,000 in there. Then he pulls out some envelopes that I hadn't thought about in years. He opens them and starts looking through the papers inside. He looks up.

"Is this the dead guy they found?" holding up the driver's license.

I nod. "Yeah, that's him."

"Do you have anything else that has to do with him?"

I shake my head no.

Eugene sat down and reached into the other case and pulled out some documents. I look and the one on top says, 'last will and testament.' He pulled it out of the stack and turned it towards me. He handed me a pen and pointed at the blank lines.

"Sign here, here and here, and…here." I do so. He takes out an ink pad. "Thumb print here," he said and pointed to a spot on the last page. After that, he gets another document. Term life insurance policy. Sign here. After I do, he called Kenny over to sign as witness. After all is signed, he pulls out a notary kit.

"When was the last time you were in Charlotte?" Eugene said. I tell him and he writes the date on all the documents the stamps them. "Ok I'm out of here." Eugene paused on his way out the door. "Good to see you, Blaise." His taillights illuminated the street less than thirty seconds later.

I thought for sure I was dead. I didn't know exactly what they had planned but I knew I was a problem they did not need. And signing a will and a life insurance policy pretty much told me all I needed to know. You see, when I worked for Eugene there were five murders of people either at the pool hall or that were regulars there. I got an idea that they were connected somehow, and that Eugene was the connection. It was why I left, and probably the reason why he was here and gone again.

I bowed my head and silently prayed. I saw images of Saul, then my parents, and then Doug and Clay, as well as other people who I had met in my life. I kept repeating the prayer Saul had given me written on the paper in my wallet. Rich yanked me out of my thoughts.

Kenny stands over me. "Gimme your wallet." I do. He points at my wrist. "and the watch." I unbuckle it and toss it to him. He tosses them both into the kitchen.

"Blu, we are leaving," he said. "You should get out of here and don't come back. Keep your head down. I don't want to read of no dead man found drinking at a local bar." With that he throws me the bag he put everything in. "You got 1 minute to get gone ."

He set a timer I had in the kitchen on the coffee table. Kenny opened one of the bags and reached in and was pressing something inside. Then he set it in the closet, next to the furnace. He pulled some pliers out his jacket pocket and did something inside the closet. He left the door open and they turned and ran out. What do I do? Is this the way the life ends? I knew they were watching. I knew they were gonna blow up the house with me in it. I sat dazed for a second then jumped to my feet and ran outside carrying the bag. I was hoping to not get shot by one of them waiting outside..

I tripped on the stairs outside, rolled twice and,

without missing a beat, rolled onto my feet, and started running again. This time towards my car. That's when I realized my car was in front and I will not have time to get to it. I just started running down the driveway, and then a flash and boom sound that hurt my ears. I was thrown off my feet and flew about twenty feet into the air before crashing back on the stones of my driveway. My ears were ringing, and my head felt heavy. Like I couldn't clear it to think. I rolled on my back and looking at my house I saw flames where the structure used to be. I collapsed on the rocks and tried to breathe.

As soon as my head cleared, I thought I better run. As I got up, I saw a light on the ground to my left. I ran towards it and when I got there, I saw a flashlight and its beam was aimed at a bag next to it. I looked at the bag as I picked up the light. It was a black, leather overnight bag. Suddenly, I heard sirens in the distance, and I grabbed the bag and ran into the woods behind my property.

I wasn't sure where I was running to until it hit me. I stopped to consider my plan. The cabin. About halfway around the lake, there is a cabin that the owners visit for a few days a month. They are a couple from Charlotte. There is a chance they would be there, but I figured it was more likely they were not. I turned and ran towards the cabin.

When I got there, I checked where I thought they might hide a key and after a minute I found it. Under a ceramic goose they had in the flower bed. I went in and closed the curtains on the door. All the others were already closed. I went to the back and fell into the bed. I hadn't turned on any lights and I was not about to. I barely made any movement. I just laid there for hours trying to figure out what had happened and why. Finally, I fell asleep and didn't wake up till the next afternoon.

I stayed there the next two days and on the second day there, I heard a phone ring. I couldn't track the sound in time, and it went to voice mail. A minute later it rang again. Following the sound, I realized it was in the bag I had picked up. When I answered I heard Dom's voice.

"Blu, are you there?"

I didn't talk at first trying to figure out if I should. Not sure if he wanted me dead. Finally, I took a chance and answered.

"Yeah," I said in a low voice. "It's me."

"Where have you been? I've been calling you."

Still suspicious, I answered. "Why would you call me on this phone? Whose is it? It's not mine."

"No shit. It's mine," he said. He sounded annoyed. "Have you looked in the bag at all?"

"No, I haven't. I've been sleeping and hiding from, I don't know, everybody." I paused. "Dom, I gotta ask do you want me dead?"

"Dead? Look in the bag call me back on this number." He hung up.

I grabbed the bag and threw it on the bed. I pulled

the zipper and turned it upside down letting the contents fall onto the bed. Some envelopes fell out first, and then cash. Then more cash. A *lot* of cash. Perfectly banded stacks of hundred-dollar bills. Exactly like the ones Rich took from my safe. Then an envelope I hadn't seen before. It had a note and with it was the life insurance and will I just signed. Dom was the beneficiary of the insurance and will. I sat there for a moment as I tried to make sense of things. I pushed the cash aside to find the envelopes. There were three of them. The first two were the big, brown ones I had on Clay that Mrs. Rayburn gave me. The third was a letter-sized envelope. I opened it and there was a one-page letter inside. It was from Dom.

Blu,

It's been one hell of a year. I want to apologize for how things went down the last few days. When I couldn't contact you, I did what I thought was best for everyone. Hope that's okay. I want to thank you for being my friend. I only have a few close friends. Usually, I have to wonder if people are there because they want something, but not you. You just really like spending time with me. I had forgotten what that feels like, for that I thank you, again. You're not out of the woods, yet. Keep your head down and 3 things you do always from now on.

Always pay cash

Use prepaid phones, a lot of them.

Don't put anything in your name.

I have the proceeds of the life and house insurance for you when or if you need it. I will take out what I spent on Rich, Kenny, and Eugene.

I think everything you'll need is in the ,bag if you can figure it out. You can always call me through Rich. If you need something, call him, I'll take care of it. Good luck.

I stayed in that cabin for about a month never going outside and eating what they had in the cabinets, and what fish I caught. I never saw another person until one day they showed up. I come out of the shower to a guy pointing a gun at me. I was lucky the owner was ex-army, so he didn't get spooked and shoot me on site and he didn't call the cops. And lastly, I was lucky he recognized me.

I told him a story about my house getting blown up and I thought someone was trying to kill me. His name was Cotton and his wife Jenny was with him. They let me stay another night and helped me formulate a plan to lay low. I was surprised how nice he was to me and how good he was at planning my continued life after death. But he was special forces and had some training in laying low if needed. "Never use an ID and never talk to anyone" was what Cotton told me. The next morning as I was leaving his last words were. "You can do this for as long as you stay sharp. Get lazy or get lonely talk to someone about yourself and you will get found. Good luck Mr. Jones" he said as he shook my hand before I drove off.

At the end the day it was decided I go to South Carolina. Small town right over the border. Cheraw. I get a hotel that has weekly rate and give him extra $100 to not put me on the registration.

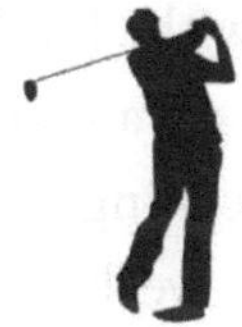

CHAPTER 18

I was there for about six months before going out to a golf course at a local state park. It was nice too. I went there in the morning hit balls and started working on my game.

I had no reason for doing it. I wasn't preparing for any competition it was just the only place I didn't need to tell anyone who I was. The only guy I ever spoke to at first was the Head Pro. And even then, I kept it all about golf.

After about 30 days a guy asked me for help on his game then another. Pretty soon, I had like a dozen people I taught regularly. Half of them were kids. I taught the kids for free and the adults I told them to pay the head pro fifty dollars for every lesson. They didn't know I wasn't getting any of it. Even the head pro laughed the first time. He came to the range and asked me about it. I just told him it was about respect.

One day I saw a guy that Saul had me contact to play a private match with. He had money and could play. We spoke and set up a match for the next week.

Pretty soon I was calling guys from Saul's list and playing 2 – 3 matches a week. I won most of them, and to be honest I was shocked I had gotten as good as I had. I was happy and got used to not talking to anyone. I hadn't been this happy with my life since my parents died.

That's when I got the phone call.

So now here I was playing golf in Cheraw and I never leave the course except to go home.

Hi. My name is Clay. Clayton Bannon is my given name, but my friends call me Race after that Race Bannon character from Johnny Quest. I play golf for a living. No, I'm not on the Tour. Those guys only have to play well for one or two weeks out of the year to stay on the gravy train. Me, I play with my own money. And I play as Saul called them "whales with skills" so I gotta bring it every day.

Now, if you'll excuse me, I gotta go. I see my next paycheck walking towards the range right now.

Oh, ya the phone call. When I heard it ring, I was scared. Shaken back to reality. I haven't gotten a phone call for months. I slowly answered it. "hello" "Blasé its

Al your godfather. We've got a problem."

THE END
FOR NOW

Printed by Libri Plureos GmbH in Hamburg, Germany